ANIMAL WELFARE *in* ISLAM

T0273136

Al-Hafiz Basheer Ahmad Masri

THE ISLAMIC FOUNDATION

Published by

THE ISLAMIC FOUNDATION

Markfield Conference Centre, Ratby Lane,
Markfield, Leicestershire, LE67 9SY, UK
Tel: 01530-244944, Fax: 01530-244946
E-mail: i.foundation@islamic-foundation.org.uk
http//www.islamic-foundation.org.uk

Quran House, P.O. Box 30611, Nairobi, Kenya

PMB 3196, Kano, Nigeria

Copyright © Compassion in World Farming, 2007/1428 AH

All rights reserved. No part of this publication may be reproduced, stored in a retrieval system, or transmitted in any form or by any means, electronic, mechanical, photocopying, recording, or otherwise, without the prior permission of the copyright owner.

British Library Cataloguing-in-Publication Data
Al-Masri, Hafiz
Animal Welfare in Islam
1. Animal welfare - Religious aspects - Islam
I. Title II. Islamic Foundation (Great Britain)
297.5'693

ISBN 13: 978–0–86037–595–1
ISBN 13: 978–0–86037–411–4 (hb)

Typeset by: N.A. Qaddoura
Cover design: Nasir Cadir
Printed and Bound in England by
Antony Rowe Ltd, Chippenham, Wiltshire

EDITOR'S NOTE

THE FIRST EDITION of this book sent ripples throughout the Islamic world. It also brought a huge postbag - mainly of an enthusiastic nature - to Basheer Masri's doorstep. He began a correspondence with many Muslims - and others - from all parts of the world.

Since his death in 1992, requests for his book have continued to come in. It is in response to those requests, and in the hope that this important work may reach an even wider audience, that this revised edition has been produced.

This scholarly book shows that concern for animals has been an integral part of Islamic teaching from the beginning. Sometimes this world-view, which sees animals as social and sentient beings who are capable of suffering, has been ignored in daily living. We hope that this book may re-ignite the flame of compassion for all beings which runs so strongly through the Holy Qur'ān and *Aḥādīth*.

PUBLISHER'S NOTE

IT IS OUR pleasure to bring out this revised edition of al-Hafiz B.A. al-Masri's important work *Animal Welfare in Islam* in collaboration with Compassion in World Farming. The appearance of this work, we believe, will help underscore the concern and compassion for animals which permeate the Islamic teachings. It is a quirk of irony that Islam, which stands for treating animals well in that like human beings they too, are the wonderful creatures of Allah, is maligned in certain quarters for its alleged anti-animal stance. In Islamic dietary code meat, no doubt, figures prominently and Muslims, cutting across their ethnic origins, have been eating meat for ages. Yet this should not be misconstrued in terms of treating animals callously. Islam exhorts that animals deserve man's care and compassion. The Qur'ān adduces animals as a sign of Allah's wonderful creative power. Several incidents in the Prophet's glorious life illustrate his considerate concern for animal welfare. Many directives of his are on record in standard *Aḥādīth* collections, which urge Muslims to be kind towards animals. Al-Masri's present work accomplishes a remarkable job in bringing into sharper focus the place animals enjoy in the Islamic scheme of things. It documents the concrete steps the Muslim polity took for the cause of animal welfare at a time when this concept was little known and hardly appreciated.

Yet it is time for Muslim society to take stock of its attitude towards animals in the light of the Islamic code on this issue. There is a pressing need for ensuring better conditions at slaughter houses in particular, and for better care of animals in general. In discharging this duty conscientiously Muslims would earn greater reward in the Next Life and, more importantly, secure Allah's pleasure, the highest felicity imaginable for them. It is time also for holding discussion on the vexed issue of stunning prior to slaughter. Let us objectively examine this issue against the backdrop of Islamic teachings, while bearing in mind the current practices and mass production of meat. This discussion assumes more significance and relevance especially in the Western countries with a sizeable Muslim population. Let us try to find ways and means for adapting our practice to the law of the land, without provoking any confrontation.

We are sure this work will achieve its twin objectives – of presenting the humane Islamic teachings on animal welfare and of drawing the attention of the Muslim community to the various nuances and dimensions of the issue of animal welfare as it figures in the West as part of the public agenda.

I take this opportunity to thank Joyce D'Silva, Ambassador to 'Compassion in World Farming' who pursued patiently and consistently this important collaborative project. I do hope our partnership will help realize our common goal of animal welfare. I must thank also my colleagues, especially Mary Barber, Naiem Qaddoura and Anwar Cara of the Islamic Foundation for their cooperation, as well as Dr. Shuja Shafi of the Muslim Council of Britain for his invaluable advice. May Allah reward them and enable all of us to engage in such pursuits which accrue to us His reward and blessings, *Āmīn.*

Leicester
Dhū al-Ḥijjah 1427H
January 2007 CE

Dr. M. Manazir Ahsan
Director General
Islamic Foundation

TRANSLITERATION TABLE

Arabic Consonants

Initial, unexpressed medial and final:

ء	ʼ	د	d	ض	ḍ	ك	k
ب	b	ذ	dh	ط	ṭ	ل	l
ت	t	ر	r	ظ	ẓ	م	m
ث	th	ز	z	ع	ʻ	ن	n
ج	j	س	s	غ	gh	هـ	h
ح	ḥ	ش	sh	ف	f	و	w
خ	kh	ص	ṣ	ق	q	ي	y

Vowels, diphthongs, etc.

Short:	ـَ a	ـِ i	ـُ u
Long:	ـَا ā	ـِي ī	ـُو ū
Diphthongs:		ـَوْ aw	
		ـَيْ ay	

بسم الله الرحمن الرحيم

CONTENTS

PREFACE

QUITE A FEW of my friends have been surprised to learn that I have chosen 'Animals' as a subject to write on from the Islamic point of view. They feel that I should be more concerned with other multifarious problems which Muslims are facing these days and for which they need help and guidance in solving. The way I look at it, however, is that life on this earth is so inextricably intertwined as an homogeneous unit that it cannot be disentangled for the amelioration of one species at the expense of another.

All human problems – physical, mental or spiritual – are of our own creation and our wounds self-inflicted. By no stretch of imagination can we blame animals for any of our troubles and make them suffer for it.

There is no paucity of Muslim scholars and theologians who are far more qualified than me to expound theologically all sorts of such problems. Notwithstanding this, I feel that my practical experience of a lifetime in the field of animal welfare, combined with some theological knowledge, lays a moral responsibility on me to express my views candidly on the current spate of cruelties to animals. The learned theologians generally remain blissfully uninformed on this subject, which is generally beyond the pale of their normal responsibilities. Similarly, the general Muslim public is not fully aware of the scale on which pecuniary, selfish and short-sighted human interests have started exploiting the animal kingdom and are playing havoc with the ecological balance.

The most alarming and distressing predicament of this deplorable state of affairs is that our Islamic countries too have started treading in the footsteps of the West in the name of commerce and trade. No doubt we have a lot to learn from Western technology and science, but surely animal welfare and environmental conservation is not one of these subjects.

The Islamic instruction and guidance on animal rights and man's obligations concerning them are so comprehensive that we need not go elsewhere for any guidance. As believers in the consummate and conclusive revelation of God, we are expected to learn from the misconceptions of the past and cast behind us the parochial approach to religion. Fourteen centuries is a long enough period to grasp mentally the fact that the way (*Dīn*) to spiritual development does not lie in ritualistic observance and the hair-splitting of the Law (*Sharīʿah*). Surely it is a long enough period to liberate ourselves from the pre-Islamic traits of our respective cultures.

Not to be cruel or even to be condescendingly kind to the so-called inferior animals is a negative proposition. Islam wants us to think and act in the positive terms of accepting all species as communities like us in their own right and not to sit in judgement on them according to our human norms and values.

I hope and pray that my Muslim brethren will fully appreciate the points I have touched upon here, after reading this book.

Although the whole of the book deals with the central theme of the welfare of animals and their relative status *vis-à-vis* man, each of the chapters has been treated as a subject on its own. Notwithstanding this, some overlapping could not be avoided. I therefore request that you do not hazard an opinion on any point before reading the complete book.

Al-Hafiz Basheer Ahmad Masri

COMMENTS AND ABBREVIATIONS

i. In Islam the dates are not given as A.D., Anno Domini, means "The year of our Lord". We prefer A.C. – Anno Christum, Christ[s] being accepted as Messenger of God rather than the Lord.

ii. S. = It is considered meritorious and obligatory for a Muslim to pronounce a reverential *Salām* whenever the name of a Messenger of God is uttered or written. 'S' stands for 'peace be upon him', in Arabic *Ṣallal-Lāhu 'alayhi wa Sallam.*

iii. A.H. = *Anno Hijrae,* i.e. the year of migration when the Holy Prophet Muḥammad[s] had to migrate from Makka to Madina in 622 A.C. This date has been established as the first year of the Islamic era.

iv. *Ḥadīth* (plural: *Aḥādīth*), i.e. words and deeds (*Sunnah*) of the Holy Prophet Muḥammad[s].

v. References = In the *Ḥadīth* and other references at the end of each chapter, the name of the book has been printed in italics.

The Qur'ānic references have been given in the text after the quotation. The first figure stands for chapter and the second for verse. In some English translations the numbers of verses may be different. In that case, please look for the verse one or two numbers above or below. In this book verse numbers have been taken from the English translation by A.Yusuf Ali; 1938; Sh.Muhammad Ashraf, Kashmiri Bazar, Lahore, Pakistan.

vi. The references to the Old and New Testaments are from The Bible (Authorised Version), University Press, Oxford, 1955.

vii. 'Muslim' means one who submits to God. Believers in Islam prefer to be called 'Muslims' and not 'Muḥammadans', nor to be known by any other names or spellings.

SAYINGS OF SOME MUSLIM SAGES

The Affinity between Man and Beast

"In the region of existing matter, the mineral kingdom comes lowest, then comes the vegetable kingdom, then the animal, and finally the human being. By his body he (man) belongs to the material world but by his soul he appertains to the spiritual or immaterial. Above him are only the purely spiritual beings – the angels – above whom only is God: THUS THE LOWEST IS COMBINED BY A CHAIN OF PROGRESS TO THE HIGHEST. But the human soul perpetually strives to cast off the bonds of matter, and, becoming free, it soars upwards again to God, from whom it emanated." (Al-Hazen)[1]

"Dying from the inorganic, we developed into the vegetable kingdom:
Dying from the vegetable, we became men.
Then what fear that death will lower us?
The next transition will make us angels.
From angels we shall rise and become what no mind can conceive;
We shall merge in affinity as in the beginning.
Have we not been told, 'All of us shall return unto Him'?" (Rūmī)[2]

CHAPTER ONE

ISLAMIC CONCERN FOR ANIMALS

Preamble

CRUELTY TO ANIMALS has existed throughout the ages. It takes various forms and guises, from cockfighting to cat burning, from sheer overloading of beasts of burden to downright neglect and abuse. Animals have died, and are dying, harsh deaths in traps and snares to provide fur coats and ornaments for the wealthy, and they have been hunted throughout the world for the sheer sport and morbid pleasure of man. However, until very recently the acts of cruelty were on a smaller and individual scale. What has changed now is the nature and extent of the cruelty, which is practised on a much subtler and wider scale. The most alarming aspect of the current streak of cruelty is that it is being justified in the name of human needs and spurious science. Scientific and pharmaceutical experiments on animals are being done to find cures for diseases most of which are self-induced by our own disorderly lifestyle.

To satisfy his ever-increasing demands and fads, man has begun to use his technological might and scientific prowess to transform increasing numbers of animals into food products. In laboratories, scientists are producing new genetic variations that may be amenable to low cost intensive methods of rearing. Many stock-keepers are more concerned with finance than the moral principles of animal husbandry, and look upon their livestock as meat and milk machines.

Even the once proud farmers have started yielding to temptation. The medieval sport of the feudal nobility to chase and kill animals for fun is still in vogue. Anglers hook up fish, and throw them back into the water maimed – just to while away their time. All kinds of denizens of the forest are fair game for the trophy-hunters. There is a large-scale carnage of fur-bearing animals. All this, and much more, is being done to satisfy human needs most of which are non-essential, fanciful, wasteful and which can be satisfied by alternative humane products which are easily available.

In this foul climate, the protests of animal welfarists are only just beginning to be heard. The politico-economic pressures of international balance of power and monetary balances of payment give little scope to state-legislators for moral considerations: and so millions of helpless animals go on suffering torture.

Why is it that human attitudes towards animals are so tardy in changing? The organised religious institutions could have played an important role in educating the general public. Almost ninety per cent of the world's population owes allegiance to one or other of the major religions. Each of these religions has the benefit of platforms wherefrom it could influence and educate captive audiences. But, one seldom hears from their pulpits any sermons preaching the word of God about animals or respect for nature. Perhaps the clerics of our religions are too busy preparing their respective laities for the Life Hereafter to spare any thought for the so-called 'dumb beasts' and the ecology which sustains us all.

Human greed and self-indulgence needed some excuse, however flimsy, to exploit animals; and the institution of religion offered them that excuse by disseminating the creed of man's unconstrained dominion and domination over the rest of God's creation. It is true that all religions have tried in their respective ways to strike an equitable balance in the mutual rights and obligations between man and the rest of the species. The Scriptures of all religions contain expostulations on all kinds of cruelty to animals, but they have ceased to be taken seriously – either by theologians or the public.

The religious institutions are supposed to be there to give guidance to their respective followers in all kinds of moral problems. If all the churches and temples, all the mosques and synagogues were to make a concerted effort to bring their moral influence to bear, it would not only educate their laities, but would also put pressure on the politicians and the economists of the world – most of whom are sitting on the fence. Perhaps some religious leaders, though, still suffer from the misconceptions of the Middle Ages when they believed that their only business was to deal with the human soul. Since animals are thought to have no soul, they are not considered to be the responsibility of organised religion.

Let us hope a day will dawn when the great religious teachings may at last begin to bear fruit; when we shall see the start of a new era when man accords to animals the respect and status they have long deserved and for so long have been denied.

MAN'S DOMINION OVER ANIMALS

Both science and religion assert that man is the apex of creation. Science bases this claim on man's physiological superiority over the rest of the animated world, while religion bases it on man's psychical excellence and potential. Islam too, declares man as the best of God's creation and designates him as His vicegerent (*Khalīfah*) on earth. So far, it all sounds very flattering, but is this position of pre-eminence unconditional? Let us see how the Islamic concept of vicegerency is meant to work. A conscientious study of this concept involves a study of issues such as:

Who is this man who has been appointed as God's representative on earth? Does anyone who possesses human features qualify for this exalted rank, or are there any qualifying conditions attached to this office? If there are any qualifying conditions, what are they?

Islam's corroboration of man's claim of superiority over the other species is circumscribed by mental, moral and physical limitations in the exercise of this power. Man should use animals out of necessity and with compassion, humility and loving care rather than with malevolence, avidity or greed for the satisfaction of creature-comforts, luxurious pleasures and self-indulgence. All the major religions have taught compassionate and humane treatment of animals. It is neither feasible nor necessary for a religion to lay down in its scriptures detailed rules and regulations covering every aspect of life. Each religion has tried in its own way to lay down the basic principles and to nurture in man a sense of responsibility as the custodian of nature. In our age of ever-increasing human mastery over nature, this responsibility has also increased proportionately.

The Qur'ān, while declaring man's vicegerency, makes it clear in the following verses, that the appointment is not unconditional:

"*He [God] it is Who made you vicegerents on earth; he who disavows, the burden of disavowal will be on him ...*" (Qur'ān 35:39)

"*Certainly, We created man in the best make.*" (Qur'ān 95:4)

However, in the very next sentence the Qur'ān makes it clear what happens to those who fail to conform to the conditions, in these words:

"*then We reduce him to [the status of] the lowest of the low.*" (Qur'ān 95:5)

Man is the only species which has been endowed with the ability to differentiate between evil and virtue and to exercise his freedom of choice. Animals are capable of differentiating between 'good and bad' in the material sense, but not in the moral and ethical sense. In the following verses, the Qur'ān tells us about those humans who misuse their freedom of choice and transgress – they lose the status of human beings in the spiritual sense and are reduced to the status of animals:

"*... they are those whom Allah has rejected and whom He has condemned and has turned into [the nature of] apes and swine, because they served evil. Such people are even worse than them and farther astray from the right course.*" (Qur'ān 5:60)[3]

No doubt such people still possess human features, as distinct from those of animals, but their moral status is degraded even lower than the status of animals for not making use of their faculties in the way expected of human beings. The Qur'ān explains this further in these words:

"*... they have hearts wherewith they fail to comprehend, and eyes wherewith they fail to see, and ears wherewith they fail to hear. They are like cattle; nay, even less cognizant of what is right. Such [humans] are far astray from the right path.*" (Qur'ān 7:179)

Again the Qur'ān urges in remonstrance:

"*And be not like those who say, 'we have heard', while they do not hearken. Verily, the vilest of all creatures, in the sight of Allah, are those deaf and dumb ones who do not use their rationality.*" (Qur'ān 8:21, 22)

The above verses occur in the Qur'ān in a context not directly related to animals *vis-à-vis* man. Nevertheless, they do lay down a very relevant principle that 'it depends on the conduct of man whether he maintains his privileged position as a human being or gets himself degenerated to a status lower than that of animals'. While elaborating man's responsibilities as the vicegerent of God, the Qur'ān lays great emphasis on the development of Godly attributes which have been imbued in man's incarnation. These attributes are eternal and unchangeable. Compassion, love, mercy, justice, charity ... are some of the Divine attributes which form the pedestal of that *masnad* on which God has seated man as His vicegerent to establish His Kingdom on earth, in harmony with His laws of nature. This Kingdom of God is not meant to be only a human domain. God's suzerainty encompasses all creation, including the Animal Kingdom. How, then, can man as His Minister on earth administer justice and grace over the whole of His Kingdom without nurturing in himself the Godly attributes and a tender conscience? This is how the Qur'ān explains this moral philosophy:

"*So, set your face to the true religion...*" (Qur'ān 30:30)

The spontaneous question arises here as to what is implied by 'true religion'. The answer is given in the lines of the same verse that follow:

> "*Direct your face towards the upright way of life – the nature created by God upon which He has instituted the innate nature of humankind. No change is permissible in God's creation; this is the proper way of life and yet, most people do not even know of this.*" (Qur'ān 30:30)

Man's superiority over other species does not lie in his physique. As a matter of fact, physically, man is inferior to animals in many respects. Muslims have often been advised by their mentors to learn lessons from some species of animals. For example, Imām 'Alī gives this piece of advice: "Be like a bee; anything it eats is clean, anything it drops is sweet and any branch it sits upon does not break."[4]

The real criterion of man's superiority lies in his spiritual volition, called in the Qur'ān *Taqwā*. This spiritual power bestows on a man a greater measure of balance between the conscious and the unconscious elements of mind, thus, enabling him to make the best use of his freedom of choice. He is considered the best of God's creation only because of this distinction. Without the power of spiritual volition, this distinction is rendered superficial.

Man's dominion over animals, in the true Islamic sense, is a patriarchal authority – an arrangement under which the paterfamilias rules the family with discipline and paternal love. The Holy Prophet Muḥammed[(s)] puts it in these words: "All creatures are like a family [*'iyāl*] of God: and He loves them most who are the most beneficent to His family."[5]

> The Holy Prophet[(s)] used to say: "Whoever is kind to the creatures of God, is kind to himself."[6]

> The Qur'ān puts this analogy in tribal or communal terms in these words:

> "*There is not an animal on earth, nor a two-winged flying creature, but they are communities like you...*". (Qur'ān 6:38)

According to the learned commentators of the Qur'ān , the word 'communities' is used here in the sense of genera, and 'animals' and 'flying creatures' of vertebra, quadrupeds, mammals, crustacea, reptiles, worms, insects and the like. They all live a life, individual and social, like members of a human commune. In other words, they are communities in their own right and not in relation to human species or its values. These details have been mentioned to emphasize the point that even those species which are generally considered as insignificant or even dangerous, deserve to be treated as communities; that their intrinsic and not perceptible values should be recognized, irrespective of their usefulness or apparent harmfulness.

To define further what it means by 'communities of animals', the Qur'ān explains:

> "*Allah has created every animal from water: of them there are some that creep on their bellies; some that walk on two legs; and some that walk on four...*" (Qur'ān 24:45)

The first category includes all kinds of worms, reptiles, centipedes, insects and all kinds of creeping creatures. The second category includes birds and human beings; and the third category covers most species of mammals. The significant point to note is that, physically, man has been put in the same bracket as all other species. The following *Ḥadīth* leaves no ambiguity in the sense in which the Qur'ān uses the word 'communities':

> "Abū Hurayrah reported the Prophet(s) as telling of an incident that happened to another prophet in the past. This prophet was stung by an ant and, in anger, he ordered the whole of the ants' nest to be burned. At this God reprimanded this prophet in these words: 'because one ant stung you, you have burned a whole community which glorified Me'."[7]

The Islamic laws (*Sharī'ah*) concerning the rights of animals are very elaborate and explicit. In the case of the ants' nest the following Juristic Rule would apply: "Any damage or a damaging retaliation for a damage is forbidden." (*Lā ḍarara wa lā ḍirār*).[8]

There are parents in this world who are cruel to their children and rulers who exploit their subjects. Similarly, there are, and will always be, people who take the concept of man's dominion over animals as a licentious freedom to break all the established moral rules designed to protect animal rights. Imām 'Alī has this to say about such people:

> "The worldly-minded people are like barking dogs and wild beasts; some of them roar on others, the strong ones eat the weak and the big ones hurt the small." And again, writing of those who misuse their authority over the weak, he writes: "A savage and ferocious beast is better than a wicked and tyrant ruler."[9]

The following verses of the Qur'ān apply verbatim to those people of our age who are exploiting wastefully the resources of nature and are wreaking havoc in the animated as well as the inanimated world, while defending their actions with clever and seemingly convincing arguments:

> "*And of mankind there is he whose glibness on the mundane life may dazzle thee, [especially] when he calls on Allah to witness the verity of his statements, because he is very skilful in his arguments.But, whenever he comes to power, he goes about in the land trying to create disorder by destroying tilth and progeny.And when it is said to him, 'fear God', his vainglory seizes him in his sin. So, Hell shall be his reckoning – verily, it is a vile abode.*" (Qur'ān 2:204-206)

In the context of these verses, the expression 'destroying tilth and progeny', means the 'resources of nature'. Literally, tilth means flora and progeny means fauna.[10]

ANIMALS' PLACE IN NATURE

The question of man's responsibilities towards animals cannot be studied without discussing the reasons for man's ill-treatment of animals. At the same time, the problem has to be understood in the perspective of the inter-relationship between man and the rest of the animated world as well as their inter-dependence upon each other. This relationship is primarily influenced by man's concept of the status of animals which man gives to them in the hierarchy of various species. To establish in our minds the status of animals is as important a postulate as is the assessment of our fellow human beings for determining our mutual relationships.

We owe a great deal to modern naturalists who have sifted quite a few facts from fallacies, myths and superstitions about animals. The pioneers in this field were mostly the members of the Christian Holy Order in the 17th century who were enthusiastic and bold enough to re-interpret the Biblical chronology of creation, in spite of being accused of and censured for puritanical leanings as naturalists. Notwithstanding the fact that some of their observations and theories have been found to be fallacious, it has been mostly due to their pioneering work that research in Natural History and Science has been given respectability and scholastic interest. As a result, we now know so much more about the animal world, its behaviour, its classification and categorization – most of all, its correlative status *vis-à-vis* the human world. The Naturalists have also helped us a great deal in understanding better those parts of our scriptures which deal with subjects, such as:

(a) Balance in Nature. (b) Conservation of Species. (c) Animals' Faculty of Speech. (d) The Utility-value of Animals. (e) The Metaphysics of Animal Mind. (f) Animals' Right to the Resources of Nature.

The Qur'ān and *Ḥadīth* have discussed all the above subjects in great detail. However, until recently, few scholars felt any need to study them seriously. Some of those who did, were not interested enough to comprehend their full significance. It is only now, when modern scientific research has started corroborating the Qur'ānic statements, that Muslim theologians have begun to give serious thought to the current problems related to animals.

a. Balance in Nature

All the sources of Islamic instruction, especially the Qur'ān, lay great emphasis on Nature Study in order to understand life as one homogeneous organism. The Qur'ān is full of verses exhorting man to study nature – the planetary system; the terrestrial elements; the fauna and flora on earth. The real purport of this repeated appeal in the Qur'ān is to give credence to the existence of Godhead as the primeval originator of the universe; but the point that concerns us here is that the creation of animals takes a very prominent place in such citations as His portents. Here are a few of the numerous such verses:

> "*Human beings and the wild and domestic animals are too, comprised of various colours. Thus, only those among His creatures who humble themselves unto God, are truly the people of knowledge.*" (Qur'ān 35:28)

> "*Verily! In the heavens and the earth, there are portents for the believers. And in your own creation, as well as in the creation of all the animals pervading the earth, there are portents for those who believe.*" (Qur'ān 45:3, 4)

> "*Behold! Everything We have created is in due measure and proportion.*" (Qur'ān 54:49)

> "*Allah knows what every female bears and by how much the wombs may fall short [of gestation], and how much they may increase – for with Him everything is in due measure and proportion.*" (Qur'ān 13:8)

Two words in the last verse are significant. The Arabic word *Unthā* denotes a female of any species, whether human or animal. Secondly, the Arabic word for measure is *'Miqdār'*, which is used in all such verses. It means 'in accordance with the particular purpose for which a thing has been created, the exigencies and the role which it is meant to play within God's plan of creation.[11]

> "*And the earth – We have spread out its expanse and cast on it mountains in stable equilibrium, and caused life of every kind to grow on it, justly weighed.*" (Qur'ān 15:19)

> "*We created man, and gave him the faculty of speech. The sun and the moon rotate in ordered orbits, the plants and the trees, too, do obeisance. The firmament – He raised it high, and set the balance of everything, so that you [mankind] may not upset the balance. Keep up the balance with equity, and fall not short in it. And the earth – He spread it out for all living beings: with its fruits, blossom-bearing palms, chaff-covered grain, and fragrant plants. Which, then, of the bounties of your Lord will you deny?*" (Qur'ān 55:3-13)

The following saying of the Holy Prophet Muḥammad[(s)] shows how much importance was attached to the conservation of nature:

> "[Even when the world is coming to an end] On Doomsday, if anyone has a palm-shoot in hand, he should plant it."[12]

b. Conservation of Species

Thanks to modern scientific research, we have started appreciating the fact that the ecological and environmental balance of our planet is of paramount importance for life on earth. This balance rests on very complex and interwoven laws of nature. The denizens of the forest, if left on their own, generally adapt themselves to those laws and learn to abide by them. One seldom sees environmental damage being done by animals living in their natural habitats, such as in the tropical forests. It is only the human species who have the idiosyncracy to flout those laws and to upset the balance of nature. And it is the humans, of all the species on earth, who need to have religious and secular education to make them realise that they are here to harness nature instead of leaving behind them a trail of wanton destruction for posterity.

Contrary to certain scientific theories, the Islamic concept is that, in this Divine design of animated nature, there are some fine differences providentially created and preserved in the origin of species to keep them distinct one from the other. Territorial, climatic and other such evolutionary processes may change their ethological characteristics or anatomical structures. In their struggle for existence, animals may learn how to camouflage themselves to distract attention or to deceive by impersonation and manipulation of their environment; but no species can transgress beyond the orbit of its genetic origin.

Wherever the Qur'ān speaks of creation, it speaks of it in terms of opposite pairs. According to the Qur'ān, not only animal life, but also every kind of flora has been created in male and female sexes. We know it scientifically now that plants, like animals, possess generative organs, i.e. male stamens and female pistils – comprising ovary, style and stigma. Botanical definitions explain stigma as that part of the style or ovary-surface that receives pollen in impregnation. Style is defined as the narrowed extension of the ovary which supports the stigma.

Keeping in mind that the Qur'ān was revealed more than fourteen centuries ago, it could not have been clearer in expression on such scientific subjects. The following verses emphasize the salient point that each species has been conditioned biologically to procreate in order to continue its heterogeneity and, thus, to go on playing its assigned part in the theatre of nature. Our scientific dexterity can bring about genetic mutations, but we shall never be able to CREATE even one germ-cell. Once a particular species is exterminated, its germ-cell is launched into eternity – as dead as the dodo – and no human skill can re-create it. Recently some scientists have expressed hopes that they might be able to bring back to life those extinct species whose dead bodies still contain some live tissues. Even if they do succeed in doing that, the fact still remains true that the re-generation of those extinct species would be dependent on the tissues containing the germ-cells which were originally created by God. The following verses of the Qur'ān bring out the significance of the law of parity in nature and, hence, the significance of an uninterrupted sequence of species:

"*Glory be to Him Who created all the progenetive pairs of that which the earth grows; and of themselves [human beings], too; and of that which they do not know [yet].*" (Qur'ān 36:36)

"*And all things We have created in pairs, that you may reflect.*" (Qur'ān 51:49)

"*[My Lord is He] Who spread out for you the earth like a carpet; and made paths therein for you, and sent down water from the cloud. Then, thereby, We have produced diverse pairs of plants – each distinct from the other.*" (Qur'ān 20:53)

"*And We cause flora of every kind to grow as spouses.*" (Qur'ān 31:10)

"*And it is He who spread out the earth... and of all fruit He produced therein, as spouses of two and two...*". (Qur'ān 13:3)

"*[God is] The Originator of the heavens and the earth. He has created mates for you from among yourselves, and mates of the cattle too, multiplying you thereby...*" (Qur'ān 42:11)

"*And He did create in pairs – male and female.*" (Qur'ān 53:45)

The story of Noah's Ark is well known. The Qur'ān tells it in Chapter 11, Verses 36-48: When the deluge came and the flooding of the whole area was imminent, there was the danger that some of the species of animals and birds might be exterminated. Even at such a time, God showed His concern to save at least one pair of each species, along with the faithful followers of Noah[(s)] by giving him the following instructions:

> "*... load in the Ark two of all species – one male and one female of each kind...*" (Qur'ān 11:40)

All these observations of the Qur'ān lay down two basic principles. Firstly, that the preservation of species is of paramount importance. Secondly, that the Divine scheme of regeneration works through the opposite, but complementary, forces of nature – not only in animals and plants, but also in inorganic matter. In the elements of nature, for example, we find that every atom possesses a positively charged nucleus of protons and negatively charged electrons. Similarly, electricity needs the positive and the negative currents to produce energy.

The underlying message in the following verses seems to be that 'every individual species, including the human species, has been endowed with a potential nature to serve the whole creation as a homogeneous unit':

> "*Behold! In the heavens and the earth there are portents for the believers. And in your own animated nature, as in that of the beasts which He has dispersed about, there are portentous messages for a people who would accept the truth.*" (Qur'ān 45:3, 4)

> "*And among His portents, is the creation of the heavens and the earth, and all the beasts that He has dispersed therein; and He has [also] the power to gather them to Himself whenever He wills.*" (Qur'ān 42:29)

The Arabic word *Dābbatun* used in this verse comprehends all breathing creatures on the protoplasmatic basis of life. In various other places also the Qur'ān has placed all kinds of beasts, amphibians, vertebrates, invertebrates, and primates (including human beings) in one bracket; and mentions the creation of all of them as one of the portents of God. This shows the importance that God attaches to life as a whole.

c. Faculty of Speech

Animals are not inferior to us because they have a different vocal apparatus; nor does the fact that they cannot make articulate speech, like we can, mean that they are 'contemptible dumb animals'. Science has proved now that they do communicate not only with each other but also with humans – at least enough to express their social interests and biological needs. Those of us who enjoy the privilege of a loving and caring relationship with our pets will bear witness to this fact. Modern scientific research by naturalists has discovered quite a few interesting facts in this field. The honey-bee's buzzing dance is not just an outburst of merriment. It is meant to convey to other bees the location of the nectar – with the exact details of direction, distance and, perhaps, the quality and quantity of the find. The insignificant ants' well-organised and industrious social life could not be run without intelligent communication among them. The sonic vibrations made by marine mammals, generally called whale-songs, are articulate communications. Animals and birds in the wild can pass on different kinds of information to each other by slight modulation of voice. The very accentuation in the 'meow' can tell the owner of a cat whether it is 'requesting', 'complaining', or saying 'thank you'.

There are numerous legends about the Muslim saints and other holy men who could talk to animals. However, for lack of authentication, they are taken generally as mere fables. There is one statement in the Qur'ān, though, which proves that man had acquired the lore of speech with animals as early as the time of King Solomon. Perhaps in those days human civilisation was more in tune with nature than it is today. The Qur'ān verse runs like this:

> "*And Solomon was David's heir, and he said: 'O ye people! We have been taught the speech of birds...'*" (Qur'ān 27:16)

d. The Utility-Value

The Qur'ān and *Ḥadīth* also plead for the cause of animal rights by repeatedly citing their utility-value and worth. Their status *vis-à-vis* human beings has already been discussed. The plea on the ground of their utility is, perhaps, addressed to those people whose values are determined more by benefit motives than by moral conscience. Here are some of many such quotations:

> "*And He has created cattle for you: you get from them your warm garments and other benefits, and you eat of their produce. And you pride yourselves on their beauty as you drive them home in the evenings, and as you lead them forth to pastures in the mornings. And they carry your heavy loads to places where you could not otherwise reach save by laborious strain to yourselves. Verily! Your Sustainer is most kind – a Dispenser of grace. And [He has created for you] horses, mules and donkeys for riding as well as for adornment – and He will yet create things of which you have no knowledge now.*" (Qur'ān 16:5-8)

> "*And surely there is a lesson for you in cattle: We provide you with a drink out of that [substance] which is in their bellies – coming from a conjunction between the contents of the intestine and the blood – milk which is pleasant for those who drink it.*" (Qur'ān 16:66)

The Arabic word *'farth'* means that glandular protoplasm which is filled with particles of secretions no longer needed by the metabolism, which is secreted out by the body. It has been established by scientists now that milk is a mixture of those particles and life-blood. The messages of some of the above verses are repeated below for emphasis:

> "*And surely there is a lesson for you in cattle. We provide you with a drink out of their bellies; and there are numerous other uses in them for you; and*

you get your sustenance out of them. And on them, as on ships, you make your journeys." (Qur'ān 23:21, 22)

"*It is God Who provided for you all manner of livestock, that you may ride on some of them and from some of them you may derive your food. And there are other uses in them for you to satisfy your heart's desires. It is on them as on ships, that you make your journeys.*" (Qur'ān 40:79, 80)

While enumerating the wonders of God's creation, the camel – the ship of the desert – is pointed out conspicuously in these words:

"*Do they not reflect on the camels, how they are created?*" (Qur'ān 88:17)

e. The Metaphysics of the Animal Mind

Unfortunately modern scientific research has been confined mostly to the behaviour and physiology of animals. Until recently, in the field of consciousness research, most scientists attributed animal learning purely to instinct. Research work in this field tends to state that no creature other than humans has been endowed with a conscious mind and, hence, has no faculty for higher cognition. This presumption is based on the misconception that even rudimentary spiritual awareness can emanate only from a consciously analytical mind as opposed to the organic life of a body which can exist and grow without the help of apprehensive senses.

What is overlooked in this hypothesis is the fact that the quantum of balance in the conscious and the unconscious elements is of varying degrees in each species. Our scientific research has not yet been able to define the lines of demarcation between the conscious, the unconscious and the subconscious elements of mind, nor have we heard the last word on how these elements interact – hence the confusion about the psyche of animals which ranges from one extreme to the other in the hierarchy of species.

Some creeds have raised them to the sublime position of being capable of receiving human souls; others have deified some animals to a status worthy of worship; while for some, all creatures other than humans are nothing more than food-parcels of flesh and bone, neatly wrapped up solely for the benefit of man. The last view is accepted mainly by those who conveniently find in it a licentious freedom to exploit the defenceless creatures for sadistic pleasure or for gain.

According to the Qur'ānic theology, all living creatures possess a non-physical force of spirit and mind which, in its advanced form, we call 'psyche'. This concept should not be confused with the concepts of 're-incarnation' or 'trans-migration' of souls, which doctrines are based on postulations different from those of Islam. Although animals' psychic force is of a lower level than that of human beings, there is ample evidence in the Qur'ān to suggest that animals' consciousness of spirit and mind is of a degree higher than mere instinct and intuition. We are told in the Qur'ān that animals have a cognisance of their Creator and, hence, they pay their obeisance to Him by adoration and worship. Out of the many verses on this proposition, the following few must suffice here:

> "*Seest thou not that it is Allah Whose praises are celebrated by all beings in the heavens and on earth, and by the birds with extended wings? Each one knows its prayer and psalm, And Allah is aware of what they do.*" (Qur'ān 24:41)

It is worth noting the statement that 'each one knows its prayer and psalm'. The execution of a voluntary act, performed consciously and intentionally, requires a faculty higher than that of instinct and intuition. Lest some people should doubt that animals could have such a faculty, the following verse points out that it is human ignorance that prevents them from understanding a phenomenon like this:

"*The seven heavens and the earth and all things therein declare His glory. There is not a thing but celebrates His adoration; and yet ye mankind! ye understand not how they declare His glory...*" (Qur'ān 17:44)

It is understood that the inanimate elements of nature perform the act of worshipping God without articulate utterances. They do it by submitting themselves (*Taslīm*) to the Divine Ordinances known as the Laws of Nature. The following verse tells us how all the elements of nature and all the animal kingdom function in harmony with God's laws; it is only some humans who infringe and, thus, bring affliction on themselves. The Qur'ān dwells on this theme repeatedly to emphasise the point that man should bring himself into harmony with nature, according to the laws of God – as all other creation does:

"*Seest thou not that unto Allah payeth adoration all things that are in the heavens and on earth – the sun, the moon, the stars, the mountains, the trees, the animals, and a large number among mankind? However, there are many [humans] who do not and deserve chastisement...*" (Qur'ān 22:18).

The laws of nature have respect for no one and 'time and tide wait for no man'. Even the most unruly and the unsubmissive have to submit to those laws, whether they like it or not – as the Qur'ān tells us:

"*And unto Allah prostrate themselves [in submission] whosoever are in the heavens and on earth, whether willingly or unwillingly, as do their shadows in the mornings and evenings.*" (Qur'ān 13:15)

The analogy of shadows is employed here to emphasise the point that man's submission should be like that of their shadows, which fall flat on the ground in the mornings and evenings – the times of the day when shadows are at their longest.

In the case of animals, however, the Qur'ān tells us that God actually communicates with them, as the following verse shows:

> "*And your Lord revealed to the bee, saying: 'make hives in the mountains and in the trees, and in [human] habitations'.*" (Qur'ān 16:68)

It is anybody's guess what form God's communication with animals takes. We know only this, that the Qur'ān uses the same Arabic word *Waḥy* for God's revelation to all His Prophets, including the Holy Prophet Muḥammad[s], as it uses in the case of the bee. It is obvious that the connotation of God's revelations to His Messengers would be different from that of His revelations to animals. This is a serious theological subject which cannot be dealt with here. Nevertheless, it proves the basic fact that animals have a sufficient degree of psychic endowment to understand and follow God's messages – a faculty which is higher than instinct and intuition.

According to a great Confucian sage, Hsun-Tzu, who lived in the third century B.C., all living creatures between heaven and earth which have blood and breath must possess consciousness.[13] Similarly, the very cognisance of human relationship with the rest of the species in Buddhist literature and the Hindu Vedānta is based on the premise that all living creatures (*jiva*) possess the faculties of thinking and reasoning (*Manas*)

f. Rights in the Resources of Nature

Once it has been established that each species of animals is a 'community' like the human community, it stands to reason that each and every creature on earth has, as its birth-right, a share in all the natural resources. In other words, each animal is a tenant-in-common on this planet with human species. Let us see now why some human beings do not act according to the terms of this joint tenancy. The inequitable attitude of some people towards animals seems to be a legacy from the early ages when man had to compete with them for food in order to survive. Man has always been in competition with animals for food, and the problem has been aggravated in the current world-situation, especially because of modern agrarian mismanagement. The Qur'ān has tried to allay this fear of man by reassuring him that God is not only the Creator but also the Sustainer and the Nourisher of all that He creates. However, the Qur'ān lays down the condition that human beings, like all other creatures, shall have to work for their food; and that their share would be proportionate to their labour. The following verse serves as the maxim for this principle.

> "*And that man shall have nothing, but what he strives for.*" (Qur'ān 53:39)

In the following verse this stipulation is repeated in the words: 'those who seek', with the additional proviso that God provides according to the needs of the people:

> "*And [God] bestowed blessings on the earth, and measured therein sustenance in due proportion...; in accordance with the needs of those who seek.*" (Qur'ān 41:10)

The conditions laid down in the above two verses for human beings to work for their food seems to be conveniently ignored by some people. Some tend to rely solely on God's beneficence – lying down on their backs with their mouths open and waiting for the manna from heaven to fall therein. Others have invented dubious ways and means to get more than their share by as little work as possible. Some of those who do work, muscle in to poach on others' preserves – and who can be an easier prey for exploitation than the poor defenceless animals who cannot fight back for their rights?

Those who expect to be fed by God, the Sustainer, without working for their bread fail to understand the real sense of the doctrine of 'pre-destination', or 'fate' (*Qaḍā' wa Qadar* or *Qismah*). The literal meaning of 'pre-destination', in the Islamic sense is: "pre-fixing the fate of some one or some thing" in the sense of determining the capacity, capability, endowment, function and other faculties. The Qur'ān uses the Arabic word *'taqdīr'* meaning 'destiny' even for the decreed orbits of the planetary motions, but also for inorganic substances as well as for animated creatures including human beings. Within those pre-fixed limitations, however, conditions could be changed for the better: suffering could be avoided or lessened by human effort and skill.

Unlike some human beings, animals are quite capable of satiating their hunger and of procuring all their necessities of life, if man would only let them do so without interference. The Qur'ān repeatedly hammers home the fact that food and other resources of nature are there to be shared equitably with other creatures. Below are just a few of the numerous such verses:

> "*Then let man look at his food: how We pour out water in showers, then turn up the earth into furrow-slices and cause cereals to grow therein – grapes and green fodder; olive-trees and palm-trees; and luxuriant orchards, fruits and grasses...*"

Let us stop at this point of the quotation and ask ourselves the question: 'what for and for whom has this sumptuous meal been laid out?' The last line of the verse tells us that all these bounties of nature are there as:

> "*Provision for you as well as for your cattle.*" (Qur'ān 80:24-32)

Again, in the following verses, the bounties of nature are enumerated with the accent on animals' share in all of them:

> "*And He it is Who sends the winds, as glad tidings heralding His mercy. And We send down pure water from the clouds, that We may give life thereby, by watering the parched earth, and slake the thirst of those We have created – both the animals and the human beings in multitude.*" (Qur'ān 25:48, 49)

In numerous passages the Qur'ān explains the reason for everything, such as: the cosmos as an ordered whole; the dark nights and the bright days; the earth with its immense expanse, shooting forth its moisture and its pastures; the stable mountains – all this, we are told, has been created for the benefit of man and animals. Below are some of such verses:

"*And do they not see that We meander water to a barren land and sprout forth from it crops, whereof, their cattle as well as they themselves eat? Will they take no notice of it?*" (Qur'ān 32:27)

We [God] brought forth from it [the earth] its waters and its pastures, and established the mountains firm – as a source of provision for you and for your animals." (Qur'ān 79:31-33)

One could get the impression from these verses that they refer only to the livestock in whose welfare we have a vested interest. After reading the whole of the Qur'ān in this context, there remains no doubt that the message comprehends all animals and not only domestic livestock. The following verses support this view:

"*There is no moving creature on earth, but Allah provides for its sustenance...*" (Qur'ān 11:6)

"*And the earth: He [God] has assigned to all living creatures.*" (Qur'ān 55:10)

In the words of Moses[s], as recorded in the Qur'ān:

"*Surely! The earth belongs to Allah; He bequeaths it to whosoever He pleases of His servants...*" (Qur'ān 7:128).

The Qur'ān recounts the history of past nations to show how they fell into error and perished. There is an incident mentioned in the Qur'ān which is relevant to the subject under discussion. The tribe of Thamūd were the descendants of Noah(s). They have also been mentioned in the Ptolemaic records of Alexander's astronomer of the 2nd century A.C. The people of Thamūd demanded that the Prophet Ṣāliḥ(s) show them some sign to prove that he was a prophet of God. At that time the tribe was experiencing a dearth of food and water and was, therefore, neglecting its livestock. It was revealed to the Prophet Ṣāliḥ(s) to single out a she-camel as a symbol and ask his people to give her her fair share of water and fodder. The people of Thamūd promised to do that but, later, killed the camel. As a retribution, the tribe was annihilated. This incident has been mentioned in the Qur'ān many times in different contexts. (Qur'ān 7:73; 11:64; 26:155; 54:27-31)

This historic incident sets forth the essence of the Islamic teachings on 'Animal Rights'. Depriving them of their fair share in the resources of nature is so serious a sin in the eyes of God that it is punishable by punitive retribution. In the case of Thamūd, this retribution was so severe that the whole tribe was annihilated for this and other iniquities.

THE SERVITUDE OF ANIMALS

Almost all religions allow the use of animals for necessary human needs. Man has always used them and their labour just as human beings take each other in service. There seems to be nothing wrong in this arrangement, except that the animals are not capable of protecting their rights as human labour unions can do. The protection of animal rights is left mainly to human conscience, social censure and government legislation; though the last does not count much, as the legislation always follows the trends of public opinion. Political leaders and reformers are two different species.

All religions have tried to regulate the use of animals humanely and with equity and justice. There are many laws in the Scriptures which cover specific cases; but the problem is that human needs and social conditions are constantly ringing the changes. Modern scientific and technological revelations, the current inter-lacing of global cultures, international and politico-economic pressures and numerous other influences are demanding modulation in our respective lifestyles. Our social and moral values are changing so fast that an average man is no longer sure how to act.

In this section the following subjects will be discussed from the Islamic point of view: Medical and other experiments on animals; Modern Hunting and Fishing for sport; Animal Fights; Beasts of Burden and other similar controversial fields.

THE ISLAMIC JURISTIC RULES

Most of the above-mentioned issues did not exist about fourteen centuries ago and, therefore, there was no occasion to pass any specific laws about them. It was felt sufficient to lay down general principles as guidelines. In cases like these, Islamic jurisprudence (*fiqh*) has left it to the Muslim Jurists (*fuqahā'*) to use their judgement by inference and analogy. The first source of Islamic law is the Qur'ān. The second source is Tradition (*Ḥadīth*). The third is consensus (*Ijmā'*). The fourth is inference by analogy (*Qiyās*), and the fifth is exercise of judgement (*Ijtihād*). Since *Ijtihād* will be quoted in many cases below, a brief explanatory note is called for here.

With the expansion of Islam into vast empires there grew the need for law and justice by inference and analogy in cases which were not mentioned specifically in the Statutory Law of the Qur'ān and *Ḥadīth*. During the early period of this development, the Muslim jurists were greatly influenced by Latin terms: '*jurisconsults*' or '*prudents*' were named in Arabic '*fuqahā'*' (plural of *faqīh*): the '*responsa prudentium*', meaning 'answers to legal questions' were named '*qiyās*' in the sense of 'legal opinions' based on analogical deductions from the Qur'ān and *Ḥadīth*. Some such 'opinions' by the jurists came to be accepted as 'canons' (*Fatāwā*, plural of *Fatwā*) – similar to what is known in Roman law as '*jurisprudentia*' or '*responsa*' or 'case law' in the West. The Roman freedom of 'opinion' based on equity, in spite of the rescript of Hadrian, had originated from secular concepts and did not meet the theological requirements of Islam. It was, therefore, found necessary to codify the Islamic law into a reliable system which would be more in line with the spirit and intention of the Qur'ān and *Ḥadīth*. The system is known in Islam as 'law by *ijtihād*'. *Ijtihād* literally means 'to try hard to do or achieve something'.

The institution of *ijtihād* has long been an issue of debate and discussion among Muslims. This is mainly due to the fear that the admissibility of the *ijtihād* law could be used by some unconscientious theologians to take liberties with the spirit and intention of the law of *Sharī'ah* to suit their convenience and transitory exigencies. Others, however, feel strongly that a total rejection of *ijtihād* would close the doors for Muslims to make the necessary adaptations according to the changing conditions of life. This whole disputation could be resolved without much fuss if a fundamental principle of Islamic jurisprudence were to be understood. It is that: the law by analogy and inference (*ijtihād*) is subordinate to the intrinsic spirit and intention of the laws of the Qur'ān and *Ḥadīth* – just as the *Ḥadīth* is subordinate to the Qur'ān . In fact the jurists of the early Islamic era followed this principle and built up juridical miscellanea which have been used for centuries and have been called case-law or 'Juristic Rules' (*qawā'id fiqhiyyah*).

Any juristic opinion which does not conform to the *Sharī'ah* law, or even does not conform to its spirit and intention, would be rejected on the grounds of the above-stated principle.[14]

EXPERIMENTS ON ANIMALS

To kill animals to satisfy the human thirst for inessentials is a contradiction in terms within the Islamic tradition. Think of the millions of animals killed in the name of commercial enterprises in order to supply a complacent public with trinkets and products they do not really need. And why? Because people are too lazy or self-indulgent to find substitutes. Or to do without. It will take more than religious, moral, or ethical sermons to quell the avidity and greed of some multi-million corporations and their willing customers.

Many of the experiments that are being done in the name of research and education are not really necessary. This kind of knowledge could easily be imparted by using charts, pictures, photographs, computer simulations, dummies or the corpses of animals that have died their natural death. In other spheres animals are poisoned, starved, blinded, subjected to electric shocks or similarly abused in the alleged interests of science. Scientists generally scoff at religionists as sticklers for convention. Are scientists themselves doing any better by sticking to their primordial practices even when there are so many alternatives available now? It is very sad to see that even in the Islamic countries where Western curricula have to be followed in science subjects, similar unnecessary and inhuman experiments are being performed on animals. Those Muslim students are perhaps in ignorance of the fact that such experiments are in violation of Islamic teachings. Even if they were aware of it, it is doubtful whether they would have any sway in the matter.

Some research on animals may yet be justified, given the Traditions of Islam. Basic and applied research in the biological and social sciences, for example, will be allowed, if the laboratory animals are not caused pain or disfigured, and if human beings or other animals would benefit because of the research. The most important of all considerations is to decide whether the experiment is really necessary and that there is no alternative for it. The basic point to understand about using animals in science is that the same moral, ethical and legal codes should apply to the treatment of animals as are applied to humans.

According to Islam, all life is sacrosanct and has a right of protection and preservation. The Holy Prophet Muḥammad[(s)] laid so much emphasis on this point that he declared:

> "There is no man who kills [even] a sparrow or anything smaller, without its deserving it, but God will question him about it.[15]

> "He who takes pity [even] on a sparrow and spares its life, Allah will be merciful on him on the Day of Judgement."[16]

Like all other laws of Islam, its laws on the treatment of animals have been left open to exceptions and are based on the criterion: "Actions shall be judged according to intention."[17] Any kind of medical treatment of animals and experiments on them becomes ethical and legal or unethical and illegal according to the intention of the person who does it. If the life of an animal can be saved only by the amputation of a part of its body, it will be a meritorious act in the eyes of God to do so. Any code of law, including religious law, which is so rigid as not to leave a scope for exceptional circumstances, results in suffering and breeds hypocrisy.

According to all religions, all life, including animal life, is a trust from God. That is why, in the case of human life, suicide is considered to be the ultimate sin. The animals, however, do not possess the freedom of choice wilfully to terminate their own life and have to go on living their natural lives. When man subjects an animal to unnecessary pain and suffering and thus cuts short its natural life, he figuratively commits a suicide on behalf of that animal and a spiritual part of his own self dies with the animal. Most problems and wrangles about the use of animals in science as well as about their general treatment would become much easier to solve if only we could acknowledge the realism of nature and learn to treat all life on earth homogeneously without prejudice and selective standards.

Take, for example, a high-security jail where cut-throats, murderers, rapists and other hardened criminals are imprisoned and compare it with a so-called research laboratory where innocent and helpless animals are cooped up in cages. By what stretch of imagination can we justify the difference in the living standards of these two places? What moral or ethical justification is there for the difference in their treatments? In the case of human prisoners you are not allowed even to prick a pin in their flesh; while the animal captives are allowed to be lacerated and hacked by surgical knives in the name of science and research most of which is for futile commercial purposes. These and many other such disparities are being allowed in our human and so-called humane societies only because of the double standards of our moral and ethical values. The real and ideal approach to this problem would be to set forth for ourselves the criterion that any kind of medical or scientific research that is unlawful on humans is unlawful on animals.

HUMAN NEEDS AND INTERESTS (*AL-MAṢĀLIḤ*)

It has been mentioned earlier that certain kinds of cruelties which are being inflicted on animals these days did not exist at the time of the Holy Prophet Muḥammad[s] and, therefore, they were not specifically cited in the law (*Sharīʿah*). Commercially motivated scientific experiments are one such case. We have to seek guidance on such issues by analogy and inference which is the third source of law, i.e. the Juristic Rules, based on *ijtihād*. One of the main excuses for all kinds of artful cruelties to animals is selfish interest or human needs. Let us see how Juristic Rules define 'needs' and 'interests' and judge these cases according to those definitions. The basic Juristic Rule (*qāʿidah fiqhiyyah*) that would apply to pecuniary experiments is: "One's interest or need does not annul other's right" (*al-iḍṭirāru lā yubṭil ḥaqq al-ghayr*). The question arises that there are certain needs that deserve to be regarded as realistic and that the use of animals to fulfil such needs should be legitimate and justifiable. The Juristic Rules are well defined for such cases. To begin with, needs are classified as follows:

1. The necessities (*al-Maṣāliḥ al-ḍarūriyyah*); i.e. the essential needs or interests without which life could not be sustained.
2. The requisites (*al-Maṣāliḥ al-ḥājiyyah*); needs or interests that are required for comfort from pain or any kind of distress, or for improving the quality of life.
3. The luxuries (*al-Maṣāliḥ al-taḥsīniyyah*); needs or interests that are desirable for exuberance, enjoyment, or even for self-indulgence.

It should be kept in mind that each of the above categories differs in degree, according to circumstances. These Juristic Rules can be applied to various situations of life; but, for the present, they concern us only in relation to the use of animals in science or otherwise.

Under the category (1) come the experiments which are absolutely essential for the well-being of both humans and animals and are done genuinely for medical research. The basic principles under which such experiments could be permissible are the following Juristic Rules (*al-qawāʿid al-fiqhiyyah*):

i. "That without which a necessity cannot be fulfilled is itself a necessity."[18] This rule only states an exception, and underlines the importance of making sure that the experiment is really a necessity (*wājib*). However, after leaving the door open for the unavoidable necessary cases, all sorts of restrictive and prohibitive conditions have been imposed by the following Juristic Rules:

ii. "What allures to the forbidden, is itself forbidden."[19] This rule implies that material gains, including food, obtained by wrongful acts, such as unnecessary experiments on animals, become unlawful (*ḥarām*). The following verse of the Qur'ān supports this stand when it condemns those who fulfil their needs by illicit means, in these words:

> "*Why do not their learned men and doctors of law prohibit them from saying sinful things and from eating food gained by dishonest means? Certainly it is evil what they do.*" (Qur'ān 5:63)[20]

iii. "If two evils conflict, choose the lesser evil to prevent the bigger evil)."[21]

According to this rule, even genuine experiments on animals are allowed as an exception and as a lesser evil and not as a right.

iv. "Prevention of damage takes preference over the achievement of interests or fulfilment of needs."[22] This rule lays down the principle that the advantages and the disadvantages of an experiment should be weighed from all angles.

v. "No damage can be put right."[23]

vi. "No damage can be put right by a similar or a greater damage."[24] When we damage our health and other interests by our own follies, we have no right to make the animals pay for it by inflicting similar or greater damage on them, such as by doing unnecessary experiments to find remedies for our self-induced ailments.

vii. "Resort to alternatives, when the original becomes undesirable."[25] This rule has a great bearing on the current controversy about the use of alternatives for animals in experiments, such as tissue-culture and other substitutes. Muslim experimentists should take this Juristic Rule seriously. It places a great moral responsibility on them, as well as on Muslim medical students, to find alternatives.

viii. "That which was made permissible for a reason, becomes unpermissible by the absence of that reason."[26]

ix. "All false excuses leading to damage should be repudiated."[27]

The above two rules leave no excuse for Muslims to remain complacent about the current killings of animals in their millions for their furs, tusks, oils, and various other commodities. The excuse that such things are essential for human needs is no longer valid. Modern technology has produced all these things in synthetic materials and they are easily available all over the world, in some cases at a cheaper price. In olden days, for example, furs and skins were a necessity. Even the Qur'ān mentions the animals as a source of warm clothing. (Qur'ān 16:5). However, this refers only to the skins and furs of domesticated cattle which either die their natural death or are slaughtered for food. There are millions of wild animals which are being killed these days commercially just for their furs and skins, while their carcasses are left to rot. Fourteen centuries ago Islam realised the absurdity of this wasteful and cruel practice and passed laws to stop it in the following *Aḥādīth*:

> "The Holy Prophet Muḥammad[(s)] prohibited the use of skins of wild animals."[28]

> "The Holy Prophet[(s)] forbade the skins of wild animals being used as floor-coverings."[29]

> "The Holy Prophet[(s)] said: 'Do not ride on saddles made of silk or leopard skins.'"[30]

It is important to note that the first *Ḥadīth* covers all wild animals. The reason why leopard skins have been mentioned specifically could, perhaps, be that the Holy Prophet[(s)] might have seen someone using a saddle of leopard skin. Similarly, the specific mention of floor-coverings and saddles does not mean that they could be used for other purposes.

VIVISECTION

Given the practical approach of Islam to human imperfections and inadequacies, as said before, some research on animals and the concomitant surgical operations may yet be justifiable provided that they are carried out without pain and under anaesthetics; provided that the subject animal is put to sleep before it regains consciousness; provided that the animal is not disfigured; provided that it is done honestly and truly for knowledge and not for the promotion of commercial interests; provided that the operations are done by conscientious and qualified scientists; and provided that there is no alternative to it. It is comparatively easier to keep under control professionally qualified scientists and educational institutions, although experience shows that even some of them could be tempted to abuse their professional privilege.

In view of the prevailing conditions in this field, a more uncompromising legislation would not be amiss.

According to the spirit and the overall teachings of Islam, causing avoidable pain and suffering to the defenceless and innocent creatures of God is not justifiable under any circumstances. No advantages and no urgency of human needs would justify the kind of calculated violence which is being done these days against animals, especially through international trade of livestock and meat. One of the sayings of the Holy Prophet Muḥammad(s) tells us: "if you must kill, kill without torture".[31] While pronouncing this dictum, he did not name any animal as an exception – not even any noxious or venomous creature, such as scorpions and snakes. People are allowed to kill them only if they become a threat to life or limb; and even then without torture.

Luckily, on this theme, there are quite a few of the Holy Prophet's(s) sayings. During the pre-Islamic period, certain pagan superstitions and polytheistic practices involving acts of torture and general cruelties to animals used to be common in Arabia. All such practices were condemned and stopped by Islam. The following few sayings of the Holy Prophet(s) will serve as an example:

> "Jābir told that God's Messenger(s) forbade striking the face or branding on the face of animals." The same Companion of the Holy Prophet(s) reported him as saying, when an ass which had been branded on its face passed him by: 'God curse the one who branded it'."[32]

This *Ḥadīth* is concerned with causing pain to the animal on sensitive parts of its body, as well as with the disfigurement of its appearance.

When the Holy Prophet(s) migrated to Madina from Makka in 622 A.C., people there used to cut off camels' humps and the fat tails of sheep. The Prophet(s) ordered this barbaric practice to be stopped. The temptation for the people to perform this sort of vivisection on the animals was that the juicy humps and fatty tails could be eaten while the animal remained alive for future use. To remove this avidity, he declared:

> "whatever is cut off an animal, while it is still alive, is carrion and is unlawful (*Ḥarām*) to eat."[33]

To make sure that no injury was inflicted on an animal while there was even a flicker of life in it, it was forbidden by the Holy Prophet[(s)] to molest the carcass in any way, for example: by breaking its neck, skinning, or slicing off any of its parts, until the body was dead cold. One of his sayings on this theme is:

> "Do not deal hastily with a 'being' before it is stone dead."[34]

'Umar ibn al-Khaṭṭāb used to instruct repeatedly:

> "Give time to the slaughtered 'being' till it is dead cold."[35]

Many other Muslim authorities have also given juristic opinions (*fatāwā*) to the effect that, after slaughter, time should be given for the *rigor mortis* to set in before cutting up the carcass.[36]

Another malpractice in Arabia in those days was stopped by the Holy Prophet[(s)] in these words:

> "Do not store milk in the dugs (udders) of animals, and whoever buys such animals, has the option to keep them or return them."[37]

Storing of milk in the dug was perhaps done to preserve milk longer or to beguile the prospective buyers.

Not only physical but also emotional care of animals was so much emphasised by the Holy Prophet[(s)] that he once reprimanded his wife, 'Ā'ishah, for treating a camel a bit offhandedly. 'Ā'ishah herself narrates:

> "I was riding a restive camel and turned it rather roughly. The Prophet[(s)] said to me: 'it behoves you to treat the animals gently'."[38]

The Holy Prophet(s) himself was once reprimanded by God for neglecting his horse, as the following *Ḥadīth* tells us:

> "The Prophet(s) was seen wiping the face of his horse with his gown. When asked why he was doing that, he replied: 'Last night I had a reprimand from Allah regarding my horse for having neglected him.'"[39]

The following *Ḥadīth* forbids the disfiguration of the body of an animal:

> "The Prophet(s) said: 'Do not clip the forelock of a horse, for a decency is attached to its forelock; nor its mane, for it protects it; nor its tail, for it is its fly flap'."[40]

There are many *Aḥādīth* forbidding blood sports and the use of animals as targets, some of which are as follows:

> "The Prophet(s) condemned those people who take up anything alive as a mere sport."[41]

> "The Prophet(s) forbade blood sports, as practised by the Bedouins."[42]

> "The Prophet(s) said: 'Do not set up living creatures as a target'."[43]

> "The Prophet(s) condemned those who use a living creature as a target."[44]

> "The Prophet(s) forbade an animal being made a target."[45]

> "The Prophet(s) was reported as saying: 'Do not make anything having life as a target'."[46]

"Ibn 'Umar happened to pass by a party of men who had tied up a hen and were shooting arrows at it. When they saw Ibn 'Umar coming, they scampered off. Ibn 'Umar angrily remarked: 'Who has done this? Verily! Allah's Messenger(s) has invoked a curse upon one who does this kind of thing'."[47]

"The Prophet(s) passed by some children who were shooting arrows at a ram. He told them off, saying: 'Do not maim the poor beast'."[48]

The fact that these *Aḥādīth* repeat the same sayings of the Holy Prophet(s) in slightly varying wordings show that he took the matter very seriously and repeated them again and again on different occasions in the presence of different people. Another significant point to note in this respect is that, to stop the use of animals as targets or in blood sports, the Holy Prophet(s) did the same as he did in the case of camel-humps (*ḥarām*) for consumption, according to the following *Ḥadīth*:

"God's Messenger(s) forbade eating a *jīfah* [carrion] of a bird or animal set up and shot at as a target for shooting."[49]

One might also appeal to the Islamic law (*Sharī'ah*) to oppose animals in military research in general and in the so-called wound laboratories in particular. The above-quoted *Aḥādīth*, as well as the Juristic Rules, would seem to support the view that our wars are our own problems and that we have no right to make the animals suffer for them.

There is no doubt that the Islamic prohibition against the cutting or injuring of live animals, especially when it results in pain and suffering, does apply to modern vivisection in science. We are able to support this interpretation of the Islamic teachings by referring not only to the above-quoted representative Traditions (*Aḥādīth*), but also to the Qur'ān. In the verses quoted below, we find expressed the principle that any interference with the body of a live animal, which causes pain or disfigurement is contrary to the Islamic precepts. These verses were revealed in condemnation of the pagan superstitious custom that the she-camels, ewes or nanny goats which had brought forth a certain number of young ones in a certain order should have their ears slit, be let loose and dedicated to idols. Such customs were declared by the Qur'ān as devilish acts, in these words:

> "*It was not Allah who instituted the practice of a slit-ear she-camel, or a she-camel let loose for free pasture, or a nanny-goat let loose...*" (Qur'ān 5:103).

> *"Allah cursed him [Satan] for having said: 'I shall entice a number of Your servants, and lead them astray, and I shall arouse in them vain desires; and I shall instruct them to slit the ears of cattle; and, most certainly, I shall bid them – so that they will corrupt Allah's creation'. Indeed! He who chooses the Devil rather than Allah as his patron, ruins himself manifestly.*" (Qur'ān 4:118, 119)

Animal-fights, such as bull and cock-fighting, are another kind of vivisection. The only difference is that, in this case, man does not do it himself – he makes the animals tear each other apart to provide amusement for him. Those who seek entertainment in such scenes of violence and if the sight of blood warms their own blood, would do better by watching more television. All kinds of animal-fights are strictly forbidden in Islam. Out of the numerous such injunctions, one would suffice here:

> "God's Messenger(s) forbade inciting animals to fight each other."[50]

It is interesting to note that, like the camel-humps, fat-tails of sheep and target-animals (*mujaththimah*) as stated above, the meat of animals which die as a result of fights is also declared in Islam as unlawful to eat (*Ḥarām*). For example, the Spaniards hold fiestas on special occasions to eat the bull killed by a matador. There is no room here to give the gruesome details of such bull-fights. Suffice it to say that the meat of such animals is *ḥarām* (forbidden) for the Muslims. One wonders how and why, in this day and age, such cruelties to animals are being tolerated by the civilised world. Even in England some revoltingly cruel dog-fights have been brought to light, some of which have resulted in prosecutions.

FACTORY-FARMING

Man's exploitation of animals and the resources of nature is spreading like an epidemic. The contagious influence of the West has started affecting the character and destiny of the developing countries. Formerly, in those countries, cruelty to animals used to be inflicted mostly through individual ignorance and the lack of veterinary facilities. Now it is becoming a mammonish creed of rapacious grabbing by fair means or foul. The agrarian mismanagement, referred to above, is particularly of concern to the environmentalists because of the change in our attitude to nature which has characterised the last forty years or so. This concern for nature becomes deeper when it applies to farm animals and wildlife, whose dependence on ecology is absolute. Those developing countries which have started copying the current methods of agriculture and animal husbandry should try to learn from the mistakes of the West.

Ever since the enclosure of commonly owned land, an ecologically sound system of farming had been developed in the West, based on the beneficial interaction between the animal and the soil. Thus, in the simplest rotation called the Norfolk four-course rotation, a quarter of the farm would be down to rootcrops such as the cattle food called mangolds or mangels and swedes or turnips; a quarter to barley; a quarter to clover-grass mixture and a quarter to wheat. Each year the fields would be rotated, so that the exhausting and the restorative crops would alternate for the benefit of fertility. As a field never had the same crop growing on it for two years in succession, crop weeds and pests, as well as fungus diseases were prevented from building up.

Sheep, not without cause called the golden hoof, grazed over at least half the farm each year and enriched the soil. Flocks would graze the barley and wheat stubbles as well as the clover leys after the hay crop had been taken. They were also to be seen arable-folded during the winter time on turnips. All the crop and animal by-products such as straw and manure were jealously conserved and had to be returned to the soil. A tenant-farmer could be dispossessed if he burned even a small amount of straw or sold hay off the farm. In the rotational mixed farming system, animals were related to the land – and to the benefit of both. The "rules of good husbandry" were written into every tenancy agreement and no one considered breaking them.

Today this cyclic system has been displaced by a straight line system on many farms in the Western so-called developed countries, and the costs are only now being realised, with a consequent trend to reintroduce many of the old techniques. Let us look at what happened.

Increasingly, the animals were taken off the land and reared intensively, tightly packed together in the windowless houses of factory farms. They were not allowed straw to lie on because this would mean extra labour and would in any case block the pumps that deal with the slurry effluent. The fields, devoid of livestock, were brought back into large hundred-acre blocks by the removal of hedges and trees and the filling in of ditches. Instead of a variety of cropping, the most profitable crop – barley – was grown continuously and each year an embarrassing bulk of straw burned in the field where the combine harvesters had left it. The soil structure started to deteriorate, and fertility could only be maintained by ever-increasing doses of artificial high nitrogen fertilizers until the soil, devoid of micro-life, became addicted to chemicals. Plant diseases and pests proliferated like the plagues of ancient Egypt and could only be controlled by recourse to the agricultural chemist's skill in devising toxic sprays. Weeds also were able to pose a challenge to the spray manufacturers. The weeds of old that the harvester knew – poppies, charlock and thistles – used to be kept in check by through-cultivation methods. Herbicides quickly eliminated these weeds and a new spectrum of more troublesome weeds arose, such as Shepherd's

Purse and Pierts Parsley. Wildlife disappeared from the cultivated areas, retreating to woodlands and motorway banks.

Now a host of new troubles are being studied. Scientists are asking whether there is a link between some of the diseases of modern life, particularly cancer, and forced-growth crops and forced-growth animals. In some parts of the country the water supply has been so contaminated with nitrogen run-off from fields that it is considered unsafe for life in general and for babies in particular. Rivers and streams have become septic where no aquatic life can survive. Concern about the deterioration in wildlife, especially insects, is making itself felt in the same way as the deterioration of frogs in some of the developing countries. Added to all this catalogue of concern is the growing pressure on politicians and economists from some scientists and the lay public about the welfare and protection of animals. Even the religious institutions are starting to murmur that the "Covenant" was not made with man alone, but with the non-human species also.

The politicians and economists of those Islamic countries which have started following blindfold in the footsteps of the West should ask themselves a few pertinent questions at this stage before they get their countries entangled inextricably in the Western system of farming and animal husbandry. Do these animals, upon which man has always depended for his food, have certain basic rights? For instance, the right to the companionship of their own kind, the right to an appropriate diet to keep them in health, and the right to a natural life and a painless death? If their Divine Creator gave them legs, is it not a blasphemy to shut them in crates where they are unable to walk? Are we perhaps forcing them back upon their own evolution by taking them from the fields and the hills and putting them in rows, unmoving – like rows of vegetables? In so doing, are we perhaps reversing our own evolution and becoming more bestial ourselves, unable to know right from wrong? Let us look at some of these areas of concern.

The patient dairy cow is now forced by genetics and nutritional science to yield many times more milk than her forbears did only a few years ago, and to such an extent as to shorten her productive life to about three years. Her calves which bring her into milk with their birth, are taken from her at one or two days old, artificially fed and then put into the market, probably to be bought by veal farmers. Such is the stress and trauma of the market that many of the calves pick up enteric diseases during this stage and so need medication with antibiotics on the receiving farm.

Some veal farmers rear the calves in communal pens on beds of straw, but there are still others who put the calves into narrow crates as soon as they are brought onto the farm. There they stay unable to walk, gambol or even turn round until they are ready for slaughter at about 16 to 20 weeks old. Although calves are highly social animals, they cannot touch one another and can scarcely see each other in their restrictive crates. They lie on bare wooden slats so that the dung and urine can be cleared away mechanically as slurry. Although ruminant and having a strong urge to chew the cud, they are denied any sort of roughage and so pluck the hair from their own shoulders and flanks to satisfy their appetites. Any slaughterman will tell you that the stomachs of these calves contain indigestible hair-balls. Although this cruel method of rearing calves for veal has recently been phased out in the European Union, it is still in widespread use elsewhere. Although the EU ban came into force in the year 2007 A.C., veal crates will continue to be used in other countries such as the U.S.A.

Chickens kept for egg production are packed tightly into wire cages and kept there all their productive lives crouching on a sloping wire floor. The sole purpose of their existence is supposed to be to lay eggs and they are denied any other inherited behaviour. They cannot stretch their wings out. Indeed the wing-span of a battery hen is 76 cm or thereabouts, yet five or sometimes even six are crowded into a cage. In the European Union each hen is given only 550 square centimetres of floor space, in many countries each hen has even less than this. In neither case has she enough space to spread her wings. The hens cannot scratch the ground, searching for seeds or grubs; they cannot dust-bathe; they cannot even flee from a more aggressive cage mate.

Perhaps the most offensive aspect of all this is the contempt for life which is bred into the modern farmer. Even cattle are no longer individuals but numbers in a herd. Poultry flocks are not numbered in hundreds these days but in tens of thousands. Will this contempt affect our sensibilities and eventually be extended to others of our own species? Even from the spiritual point of view, meat of such animals is unhealthy to eat. Our dieticians do not lay enough stress on the point, but the history of nations bears out the fact that there is a strong ethological link between diet and character formation. Animals reared under unnatural and inhumane conditions become frustrated, morose and cantankerous. Such characteristics are passed on to those who eat their meat, though it may take many generations to show. The biological laws of nature are the same for the human species as for other animals. Their diet, environment and general living conditions affect all of them alike. Like human beings, animals too have a sense of individuality. The Qur'ān repeatedly confirms this fact. Even chickens are individuals and, if given the chance, will demonstrate their own characters peculiar to each individual.

The writer knows of a hen who is six years old. A farmer friend of his bought her with a dozen of her sisters from a battery farm some years ago – poor, featherless, demented things. They then were unable to perch, and stared vacantly at the new experience called 'grass'. It was something out of this world for her, until taught by other freer cousins the joys of free-range. This hen, called 'One-tail', because she only ever did grow one feather in her tail, now enters the house through the cat-flap and challenges the cat to its dinner.

The emotions of animals and of human beings are, no doubt, the same, even though we may differ in our respective needs and in degree. They feel pain and joy, they fear and feel relief, they experience an advanced sense of fun – just as human beings do.

We have to ask ourselves all these and many more questions. The basic moral question is – how right is it to deny these creatures of God their natural instincts so that we may eat the end product? For Muslims these questions pose the additional question of a fundamental moral pertinence –

would our Holy Prophet Muḥammad[(s)] have approved of the modern methods of intensive farming systems if he were alive today? His overwhelming concern for animal rights and their general welfare would certainly have condemned (*La'ana*) those who practise such methods, in the same way as he condemned similar other cruelties in his day. He would have declared that there is no grace or blessing (*Barakah*) – neither in the consumption of such food nor in the profits from such trades. These are not just hypothetical questions. The cruel and inhumane methods of intensive farming are being practised in most Islamic countries these days, even in countries where indigence is no excuse.

For some years the developing countries, including the Islamic countries, have been importing high technology farming systems from the West, and the trend is growing fast. According to figures published in the "World Poultry" gazette for October 1984, European firms have developed special projects of high technology farming units for the Middle East. One of their laying houses in Egypt is producing 25 million eggs per year. According to the same gazette, similar projects have been installed in Saudi Arabia, Libya, Morocco, Tunisia, Oman and other Middle Eastern States. Pakistan, Indonesia and other Islamic countries are following suit. Under the intensive farming system, a hen lays on average over 300 eggs a year. One can imagine from the above figures how many millions of hens are being subjected to the un-Islamic methods of food production in all these Islamic countries put together.

Most of these un-Islamic businesses are flourishing in Islamic countries due to the ignorance of the consumer public. People do not know how meat chickens are being reared, how they have been bred to grow excessively fast and how they are being fed on diets to fatten them even faster to produce more meat, more quickly. Fowls and other food animals are no longer creatures of God; they are numbers in computers. After all, computers can give the breeders up-to-the-minute figures of profit and loss at the touch of a button, while God's reckoning is a long way off in the Hereafter. If only the average, simple and God-fearing Muslim consumers of such food-animals knew the gruesome details about the

Westernised meat industry in their own Islamic countries, they would become vegetarians rather than eat such sacrilegious meat. The least that the Muslim *'Ulamā'* can do is to inform the lay public how their food is being produced, so that people can – with knowledge – decide what to do about it. Some may decide that the products of intensive factory farms are not suitable, both from religious and health points of view, and seek more naturally produced eggs and meat such as free-range or organic; or give up eating meat altogether.

GENERAL REFORMS OF ISLAM

The Islamic teachings have gone to great lengths to instil a sense of love, respect and compassion for animals. As already mentioned, some of the cruelties to animals which used to be practised during and before the time of the Holy Prophet[(s)] were stopped by him. However, we come across many cruel practices these days which, though not mentioned in the Islamic law, are obviously against the very spirit of the teachings of Islam. It is sad to see that most of these cruelties are taking place in so-called civilised Western countries. However, it is encouraging to see that the protest of the Western animal welfarists against all kinds of cruel exploitation of animals is well organised and, hopefully, will prevail.

From the Islamic point of view, however, the worrying thing is that the developing countries, including most of the Islamic countries, have started emulating their Western preceptors in practices such as intensive farming methods; use of insecticides which are harmful to human and animal health and do more damage to the environment than good to crops; and export of animals in millions for exotic foods or for profit-motivated experiments to manufacture cosmetics and other such luxuries. Better and quicker returns, plus the feeling that civilised Western society has given its tacit approval to these and many other cruel methods of making money are corroding the moral ethos of the underdeveloped as well as the affluent nations of the East. Islam's directive teachings in cases like these are very helpful and educational, as the few examples given below will show:

THE MORAL APPEAL OF ISLAM

Most of the sermons from our pulpits are admonitions against sin. If someone were inclined to choose a subject pertaining to animal welfare, there is enough material in every scripture to choose from. For example, here are two sayings of the Holy Prophet Muḥammad(s) which could make very appropriate themes for such sermons. In the following sayings, the Holy Prophet(s) has placed the killing of animals without a justifiable reason as one of the major sins:

> "Avoid the seven obnoxious things [deadly sins]: polytheism; magic; the killing of breathing beings ![51] " which God has forbidden except for rightful reason."

> "The baneful [sinful] things are: polytheism; disobedience to parents; the killing of breathing beings."[52]

The Holy Prophet(s) has even tried the 'Punishment and Reward' approach in the following *Aḥādīth*:

> "The Prophet(s) told his Companions of a woman who would be sent to Hell for having locked up a cat; not feeding it, nor even releasing it so that it could feed itself."[53] (This *Ḥadīth* has been recorded by almost all the authentic books of *Ḥadīth,* as Ref. No. 53 will show.)

> "The Prophet(s) told his Companions of a serf who was blessed by Allah for saving the life of a dog by giving it water to drink and quenching its thirst."[54]

> "The Prophet(s) was asked if acts of charity even to the animals were rewarded by God. He replied: 'Yes, there is a reward for acts of charity to every beast alive.'"[55]

"Mishkāt Al-Maṣābīḥ" quoted from "Bukhārī" and "Muslim" to the effect that: 'A good deed done to a beast is as good as doing good to a human being; while an act of cruelty to a beast is as bad as an act of cruelty to human beings' and that: 'Kindness to animals was promised by rewards in Life Hereafter.'[56]

BEASTS OF BURDEN

The following *Aḥādīth* lay down the principles that animals in the service of man should be used only when necessary and for the purpose for which they are meant, and that their comfort should not be neglected:

> "The Prophet[(s)] once saw a man sitting on the back of his camel in a market place, addressing people. He said to him: 'do not use the backs of your beasts as pulpits, for God has made them subject to you so that they may take you to places you could not otherwise reach without fatigue of body.'"[57]

> "The Prophet[(s)] once passed by a lean camel whose belly had shrunk to its back. 'Fear God' he said to the owner of the camel, 'in these dumb animals and ride them only when they are fit to be ridden, and let them go free when it is meet that they should rest.'"[58]

About taking care of animals during travelling, the Holy Prophet[(s)] used to give the following advice:

> "When you journey through a verdant land, [go slow to] let your camels graze. When you pass through an arid area, quicken your pace [lest hunger should enfeeble the animals]. Do not pitch your tents for the night on the beaten tracks, for they are the pathways of nocturnal creatures."[59]

Saying daily prayers (*ṣalāt*) is one of the five most important obligations of the Muslim religion. In the following *Ḥadīth*, one of his Companions tells us that the Holy Prophet[(s)] and his fellow travellers used to delay even saying their prayers until they had first given their riding and pack animals fodder and had attended to their needs:

> "When we stopped at a halt, we did not say our prayers until we had taken the burdens off our camels' backs and attended to their needs."[60]

Imām ʿAlī's general advice about pack-animals is:

> "Be kind to pack-animals; do not hurt them; and do not load them more than their ability to bear."[61]

MENTAL CRUELTY

Islam's concern for animals goes beyond the prevention of physical cruelty to them which, logically, is a negative proposition. It enjoins on the human species, as the principal primates of the animated world, to take over the responsibility for all creatures in the spirit of a positive philosophy of life and to be their active protectors. Prevention of physical cruelty is not enough; mental cruelty is equally important. In this age of scientific research and knowledge, it should not be difficult to comprehend that these so-called 'dumb animals', too, have feelings and emotional responses. Dogs, cats and various other animals that have become part of human society as pets were originally untamed brutish animals. It was only love and care that won their confidence in man; and it is only their ill treatment and neglect by man that brings back the beast in them.

The incidents of the Holy Prophet Muḥammad's[(s)] personal grooming of his horse; his wife ʿĀ'ishah's rough handling of her camel; the Holy Prophet's[(s)] prohibition of cutting forelocks, the mane or tail; the condemnation of striking and branding on the face or ears: – all these and many other such *Aḥādīth* show that this great man Muḥammad[(s)] had realised even fourteen centuries ago that animals have a sense of adornment and sensitivity. In the following incident, a bird's emotional distress has been treated as seriously as a physical injury:

> "We were on a journey with the Apostle of God[(s)] and he left us for a while. During his absence, we saw a bird called *ḥummarah* with its two young and took the young ones. The mother-bird was circling above us in the air, beating its wings in grief, when the Prophet came back and said: 'who has hurt the FEELINGS of this bird by taking its young? Return them to her'."[62]

It is reported by the same authority that: "a man once robbed some eggs from the nest of a bird. The Prophet[(s)] had them restored to the nest."[63]

SLAUGHTER OF FOOD ANIMALS

One wonders why Islam, with all its concern for animals, has allowed its followers to consume their meat and has not asked them to become vegetarian, like some other religions. The question of vegetarianism and meatarianism will be discussed later. Let us accept the fact that Islam has allowed the slaughter of animals for food and see what instructions it gives us to ensure humane slaughter, with as little pain to the victim as possible. The following *Aḥādīth* are self-explanatory:

> "God's Messenger[(s)] was reported as saying: 'Allah Who is Blessed and Exalted, has prescribed benevolence towards everything [and has ordained that everything be done in a good way]; so, when you must kill a living being, do it in the best manner and, when you slaughter an animal, you should [use the best method and] sharpen your knife so as to cause the animal as little pain as possible.'"[64]

"The Messenger of Allah was heard forbidding to keep waiting a quadruped or any other animal for slaughter."[65]

"The Prophet[(s)] forbade all living creatures to be slaughtered while tied up and bound."[66]

"The Holy Prophet[(s)] said to a man who was sharpening his knife in the presence of the animal: 'Do you intend inflicting death on the animal twice – once by sharpening the knife within its sight, and once by cutting its throat?'"[67]

Imān 'Alī says: "Do not slaughter sheep in the presence of other sheep, or any animal in the presence of other animals."[68]

'Umar once saw a man denying a sheep, which was going to slaughter, a satiating measure of water to drink. He gave the man a beating with his lash and told him: 'Go, water it properly at the time of its death, you knave!'"[69]

It is reported that 'Umar once saw a man sharpening his knife to slaughter a sheep, while he was holding the cast sheep down with his foot placed on its face. He started lashing the man until he took to his heels. The sheep, meanwhile, had scampered off.[70]

CONCLUSION

There seems to be no better winding up of this chapter than by quoting a great Muslim theologian of the 20th century – Sayyid Abul A'lā Mawdūdī (1903-79 A.C.). This is what he says about the rights of animals and their general treatment in the light of the teachings of Islam:

"God has honoured man with authority over His countless creatures. Everything has been harnessed for him. He has been endowed with the power to subdue them and make them serve his objectives. This superior position gives man an authority over them and he enjoys the right to use them as he likes. But that does not mean that God has given him unbridled liberty. Islam says that all the creation has certain rights upon man. They are: he should not waste them on fruitless ventures nor should he unnecessarily hurt or harm them. When he uses them for his service he should cause them the least possible harm, and should employ the best and the least injurious methods of using them.

"The law of Islam embodies many injunctions about these rights. For instance, we are allowed to slaughter animals for food and have been forbidden to kill them merely for fun or sport and deprive them of their lives without necessity... Similarly, killing an animal by causing continuous pain and injury is considered abominable in Islam. Islam allows the killing of dangerous and venomous animals and of beasts of prey only because it values man's life more than theirs. But here too it does not allow their killing by resort to prolonged painful methods".

"Regarding the beasts of burden and animals used for riding and transport, Islam distinctly forbids man to keep them hungry, to take hard and intolerable work from them and to beat them cruelly. To catch birds and imprison them in cages without any special purpose is considered abominable. What to say of animals: Islam does not approve even of the useless cutting of trees and bushes. Man can use their fruit and other produce, but he has no right to destroy them. Vegetables, after all, possess life, but Islam does not allow the waste of even lifeless things; so much so that is disapproves of the wasteful flow of too much water. Its avowed purpose is to avoid waste in every conceivable form and to make the best use of all resources – living and lifeless."[71]

REFERENCES AND NOTES

1. Ḥasan ibn al-Haytham, a famous Muslim philosopher and scientist (cir. 11th century A.C.) known in Europe as 'Al-Hazen'. He belonged to the first school of Scholasticism called the 'Academy of Science and Philosophy' which was founded by Abū Ḥudhayfah Wāṣil in the early 8th century A.C. as quoted in *The Spirit of Islam*; Syed Amir Ali; 10th Edition; Chatto & Windus, London; June 1964; p.424.
2. Mawlānā Jalāl al-Dīn Rūmī – one of the most eminent 'orthodox' Muslim theologians and sages (1207-1273 A.C. = 585-651 A.H.). (As quoted in the same Ref. No. 1); p.425.
3. cf. *Ṭabarī's Commentary*, 2:65; *Manār*, 6:448; for *Ṭāghūt* in the sense of evil. Also see Rāzī.
4. *Maxims of 'Alī*; translated by al-Halal from *Nahj al-Balāghah* (in Arabic); Sh. Muhammad Ashraf, Lahore, Pakistan; p.436. (Hereafter referred to as *Maxims.*) Imām 'Alī ibn Abī Ṭālib was the son-in-law of the Holy Prophet Muḥammad(s), and the fourth Caliph (644-656 A.C. – 22-34 A.H.).
5. Narrated by Anas. *Mishkāt al-Maṣābīḥ*, 3:1392; quoted from *Bukhārī*.
6. *Wisdom of Prophet Muhammad*(s); Muḥammad Amīn; The Lion Press, Lahore, Pakistan; 1945.
7. *Bukhārī* and *Muslim*.
8. Juristic Rules serve as legal maxims in the Islamic jurisprudence (*Fiqh*).
9. *Maxims* (see Ref. No.4); pp.203, 381.
10. cf. *Rāzī* and *al-Azharī*, as quoted in *Manār* II (in Arabic); p.248.
11. *The Message of the Qur'ān*; Muhammad Asad; Dar al-Andalus, Gibraltar; 1980; footnotes 18, 19; p.359.
12. *Musnad of Aḥmad*, 5:440 and 3:184. (Hereafter referred to as *Musnad*).
13. *Basic Writings of Husn-Tzu*; Burton Watson; Colombia University Press, New York; 1963; p.106.
14. *Arabia* – The Islamic World Review; Vol.4, No.49, September 1985; Slough, England; p.11.
15. Narrated by Ibn 'Umar and by 'Abdullāh ibn al-'Āṣ. *al-Nasā'ī*, 7:206, 239, Beirut. Also recorded by *Musnad al-Jāmi'* of *al-Dārimī*; Delhi, 1337. Also *Mishkāt al-Maṣābiḥ*: English translation by James Robson, in four volumes; Sh. Muhammad Ashraf, Lahore, Pakistan; 1963 (hereafter referred to as 'Robson').
16. Narrated by Abū Umāmah. Transmitted by *al-Ṭabarānī*.
17. In Arabic: "*al-A'mālu bi'l-niyyah*".
18. In Arabic: "*Mā lā yatimmu al-wājib illā bihi, fahuwa wājib*".

19. In Arabic: "*Mā addā ilā al-ḥarām, fahuwa ḥarām*".
20. *The Meaning of the Glorious Qur'ān*; English translation by Marmaduke Pickthall; George Allen & Unwin Ltd., London; 1957; verse 63, chapt. 5.
21. In Arabic: "*Idhā ta'āraḍat mafsadatāni ru'iya a'zamahumā ḍararun bi-irtikāb akhffiahimā*".
22. In Arabic: "*Dar' al-mafāsid muqaddamun 'alā jalb al-maṣāliḥ*".
23. In Arabic: "*Al-ḍararu lā yuzālu*".
24. In Arabic: "*Al-ḍararu lā yuzālu bi mithlihi aw bi ḍararin akbaru minhu*".
25. In Arabic: "*Idhā ta'dhara al-aṣlu, yuṣāru ilā al-badal*".
26. In Arabic: "*Mā jāza li 'udhrin, baṭala bi zawālihi*".
27. In Arabic: "*Saddū al-dharā'i' al-mu'addiyah ilā al-fasād*".
28. Narrated by Abū Mālik on the authority of his father. *Abū Dāwūd* and *Tirmidhī* as recorded in *Garden of the Righteous – Riyāḍ al-Ṣāliḥīn* of Imām Nawāwī; translated by M.Z. Khan; Curzon Press, London, 1975; (hereafter referred to as *Riyāḍ*); *Ḥadīth* No. 815, p.160.
29. ibid.
30. Narrated by Mu'āwiyah. *Abū Dāwūd*; (see *Riyāḍ*, Ref. No. 28); *Ḥadīth* No. 814, p.160.
31. In Arabic: "*Lā taqtalū bi'l-īdhā*".
32. Narrated by Jābir ibn 'Abdullāh. *Muslim*, Vol. 3, *Ḥadīth* No. 2116. Also *'Awn al-Ma'būd Sharḥ Abū Dāwūd* (hereafter referred to as *'Awn*); 7:232, *Ḥadīth* No. 2547. Also *The Lawful and Unlawful in Islam* (in Arabic); Yūsuf al-Qaraḍāwī; Maktabat Wahbah, Cairo; 1977; p.293. Also *'Robson'* (Ref. No. 15); p.872.
33. Narrated by Abū Wāqid al-Laythī. *Tirmidhī*; *Ḥadīth* No. 1480, Chapt. on *Al-Aṭ'imah*. Also *'Robson'*. (Ref. No. 15) p.874.
34. *"Kitāb al-Muqnī"*, 3:542. Also "*Al-Muḥallā*", 7:457; Ibn Ḥazm; (both in Arabic).
35. *"Al-Muḥallā"*, 7:457; Ibn Ḥazm; (in Arabic). 'Umar ibn al-Khaṭṭāb was the second Caliph (634-644 A.C. = 12-22 A.H.).
36. *Kitāb al-Nīl wa Shifā' al-'Alīl*", 4:460; (in Arabic).
37. *Muslim* and *Bukhārī*. Also *Holy Traditions*; 1st Edition; Vol.1; Muhammad Manzur Ilahi; Ripon Press, Lahore, Pakistan; 1932; p.149.
38. Narrated by 'Ā'ishah. *Muslim*, Vol. 4, *Ḥadīth* No. 2593. Also *'Awn*, 7:155, *Ḥadīth* No. 2461; (Ref. No. 32).
39. Narrated by Yaḥyā ibn Sa'īd. "*Mālik ibn Anas al-Aṣbaḥī*. Also *al-Muwaṭṭa'*, (in English); Divan Press, Norwich, England; 1982; p.205.
40. Narrated by 'Utbah ibn Farqad Abū 'Abdullāh al-Sulamī. *Abū Dāwūd*. Also *'Awn*, 7:216, 217, *Ḥadīth* No. 2525; (Ref. No. 32).

41. Narrated by 'Abdullāh ibn 'Umar. *Muslim*, Vol. 3, *Ḥadīth* No. 1958.
42. Narrated by 'Abdullāh Ibn 'Abbās. *'Awn*, (Ref. No. 32); 8:15, *Ḥadīth* No. 2803. Also '*Robson*'; p.876. (Ref. No. 15, but it does not mention 'Bedouins').
43. Narrated by 'Abdullāh ibn 'Abbās. *Muslim*, Vol. 3, *Ḥadīth* No. 1957. Also '*Robson*'; p.872; (Ref. No. 15).
44. Narrated by 'Abdullāh ibn 'Umar. *Bukhārī* and *Muslim*. Also '*Robson*'; p.872. (Ref. No. 15).
45. Narrated by Anas. Recorded by Riyāḍ. (Ref. No. 28); *Ḥadīth* No. 1606; p.272.
46. Narrated by Ibn 'Abbās. *Ṣaḥīḥ Muslim – Kitāb al-Ṣayd Wa'l-Dhabā'iḥ*"; Chapt. DCCCXXII, Vol.III; Sh. Muhammad Ashraf, Lahore, Pakistan, 1976; *Ḥadīth* No. 4813; p.1079; (hereafter referred to as *Kitāb al-Ṣayd*).
47. ibid. Narrated by Sa'īd ibn Jubayr.
48. Narrated by 'Abdullāh ibn Ja'far. *Al-Nasā'ī*, 7:238.
49. Narrated by Wāqid al-Laythī. *Abū al-Dardā'*. *Tirmidhī*, *Ḥadīth* No. 1473, Chapt. *Al-Aṭ'imah'*. Also '*Robson*' (Ref. No. 15); p.874.
50. Narrated by 'Abdullāh ibn 'Abbās. *Bukhārī*, *Muslim*, *Tirmidhī* and *Abū Al-Dardā'*; recorded in *Riyāḍ* (Ref. No. 28); *Ḥadīth* No. 1606; p.271. Also '*Robson*' (Ref. No. 15); p.876.
51. Narrated by Abū Hurayrah. *Ṣaḥīḥ Muslim – Kitāb al-Īmān* (Ref. No. 46); Chapt.XXXIX, Vol.I; p.52. *Bukhārī*, 4:23. Also *'Awn*, (Ref. No. 32); *Ḥadīth* No. 2857.
52. ibid. Narrated by 'Abdullāh Ibn 'Amr.
53. Narrated by 'Abdullāh ibn 'Umar. *Bukhārī*, 4:337; recorded in *Riyāḍ* (Ref. No. 28), *Ḥadīth* No. 1605; p.271. Also *Muslim*, Vol. 4, *Ḥadīth* No. 2242. English translation by Abdul Hamid Siddiqi; Sh. Muhammad Ashraf, Lahore, Pakistan; 1976; Vol. 4, *Ḥadīth* No. 5570; p.1215. (According to the English translation, this *Ḥadīth* was also narrated by Abū Hurayrah; *Ḥadīth* No. 5573; p.1215.
54. Narrated by Abū Hurayrah. *Muslim*, Vol. 4, *Ḥadīth* No. 2244. Also *Bukhārī*, 3:322. Also *'Awn* (Ref. No. 32); *Ḥadīth* No. 2533 and others.
55. Narrated by Abū Hurayrah. *Bukhārī*, 3:322. Also *Muslim*, Vol. 4; *Ḥadīth* No. 2244. Also *'Awn* (Ref. No. 32), 7:222, *Ḥadīth* No. 2533. Also *Mishkāt al-Maṣābīḥ*; Book 6; Chapt.6.
56. *Mishkāt al-Maṣābīḥ*; Book 6, Chapt.7, 8:178.
57. Narrated by Abū Hurayrah. *'Awn* (Ref. No. 32); 7:235; *Ḥadīth* No. 2550. Also *Traditions of Islam*; Alfred Guillaume; Khayats Oriental Reprinters, Beirut, Lebanon; 1966; pp.106, 107. (Hereafter referred to as '*Guillaume*').
58. Narrated by 'Abdullāh ibn Ja'far. *'Awn* (Ref. No. 32); 7:221; *Ḥadīth* No. 2532.

59. Narrated by Abū Hurayrah. *Ṣaḥīḥ Muslim – Kitāb al-Īmān* (Ref. No. 53); Vol.III; Chapt. DCCCVII; *Ḥadīth* No. 4724; pp.1062, 1063.
60. Narrated by Anas. *'Awn* (Ref. No. 32); 7:223; *Ḥadīth* No. 5234. Also *'Guillaume'* (Ref. No. 57); pp.106, 107.
61. *Maxims* (Ref. No. 4).
62. Narrated by 'Abd al-Raḥmān ibn 'Abdullāh ibn Mas'ūd. *Muslim*. Also *'Awn* (Ref. No. 32) *Ḥadīth* No. 2658. Also 'Guillaume' (Ref. No. 57); p.106.
63. ibid.
64. Narrated by Shaddād ibn Aws. Muslim; Vol. 2; Chapt. 11; Section on *'Slaying'*; 10:739, verse 151. Also 'Robson' (Ref. No. 15); p.872. Also recorded in *Riyāḍ*. (Ref. No. 28); *Ḥadīth* No. 643; p.131.
65. Bukhārī. Also Muslim; Vol. 2; Chapt.11; Section on *'Slaying'*; 10:739; verse 152. Also 'Robson' (Ref. No. 15); p.872.
66. ibid. (Ref. No. 46); *Ḥadīth* No. 4817; p.1079.
67. *Al-Furū' Min al-Kāfi Li'l-Kulaynī* (in Arabic); 6:230.
68. ibid. (for 'Alī see Ref. No. 4).
69. Reported by Ibn Sīrīn about 'Umar and recorded in *Badā'i' al-Ṣanā'i'* (in Arabic); 6:2811.
70. ibid. 6:2881.
71. *Towards Understanding Islam;* Sayyid Abul A'lā Mawdūdī; English translation by Dr. Khurshid Ahmad, a Muslim of renown in the literary and religious circles in the West; Islamic Publications Ltd., 13-E Shah Alam Market, Lahore, Pakistan.

CHAPTER TWO

VEGETARIANISM V/S MEATARIANISM

Preamble

WE HAVE DISCUSSED in the previous chapter the Islamic exhortations for kindness to all living creatures. As a matter of fact, Islam is so concerned about compassion for animals that one wonders why it has allowed us to kill them for food and why it did not enjoin on us to become vegetarians. To find an answer to this question, one has to understand and appreciate the overall approach to the Islamic laws regulating human behaviour in relation to other animals and the environment. These laws do not lay down categorical imperatives irrespective of man's biological necessities of life, food being the most important of them.

Unfortunately the limited scope of this book does not permit a detailed discussion of the respective points of view of both vegetarians and non-vegetarians. From the humanitarian point of view, it would be an ideal situation if all the world were to become vegetarian and all the animals were allowed to live their natural lives. Perhaps a time may come, sooner or later, when this will happen. Meanwhile the poor animals shall go on having their throats slit.

Before discussing the subject from the Islamic angle, it will help to mention briefly other points of view, including those offered by other religions as well as the current scientific view that meat is not as essential and as healthy a diet as people generally consider it to be. At the same time, the writer's moral responsibility demands that the reader should know at the very outset what his personal feelings are and what to expect from this chapter.

The writer was born into a meat-eating family some 74 years ago. In those days the general impression used to be that meat was the best source of nourishment, and a child was weaned from milk to a meat diet right from the cradle. Modern information about the properties of vitamins, proteins, carbohydrates and minerals found in vegetables etc. was not available then. The concept of balance in diet was not fully understood. It was natural, therefore, that the writer's metabolism got so used to meat that a complete change over to a vegetarian diet has now become very difficult. Otherwise, at heart, he has become a vegetarian by conviction.

Those who are traditionally habituated to and indoctrinated into believing from an early age that meat is more nutritious than vegetable food find it more difficult mentally than physically to give it up. In some cases this indoctrination even takes on cultural overtones, as if meat-eating had some ethnological advantage. Then there is the problem of life-long acquired taste for meat which works as a drag even on those who wish to give it up. Very few meat-eaters realise that man's natural food is vegetables, fruit and nuts. Even his body is not equipped with the tools required for killing and eating flesh. Why then has he ended up as the most ferocious and devastating of the carnivores and a sadist – killing not only for food but for pleasure and fun as well? How has the unnatural diet of meat affected not only his own health but also the environmental equipoise of the planet which he hopes he will inhabit through the generations until eternity? What has his religion to say about this physical as well as mental pabulum and spiritual sustenance – or is he using his religion to peg on it his perverted sense of power over the rest of the species?

It is not possible in this short chapter to deal at any length with the multifarious aspects of these and other questions. The following few pages are just a laconic explanation, from biological, economic and mainly moral points of view of why the writer has come to believe that a well-balanced herbivorous diet is more nutritious, healthier and tastier than that of meat – for those who heed Cicero's advice:

"Thou shouldest eat to live; not live to eat."[1]

THE DIALECTICS OF DIET AND HEALTH

We are fortunate in our age that scientific research in dietetics has enabled us to eat a much more balanced diet than our ancestors did. We are much better informed about the properties of foodstuffs, such as proteins, vitamins, carbohydrates and other nutrients, which we can measure now in terms of calories. We know now the difference between saturated (animal) and unsaturated (vegetable) fats and their comparative cholesterol levels.

Both vegetarians and meatarians (meat-eaters) have no bone to pick with each other on the fundamental point that diet should be such as to supply adequate nutrition to the body to keep it functioning healthily. The controversy starts between them only when it comes to the choice of sources from which man can derive the nutrients. The old school of dieticians still believes that these sources of nutrition are not distributed equally in the various foods available and, therefore, a mixed diet of vegetable and meat is more likely to provide a balanced amount of all bodily needs. However, apart from moral and ethical considerations of cruelty to animals which the current meat-eating habits entail, scientific opinion is shifting more and more, for physiological reasons, towards a purely herbivorous diet. It is being claimed now by reliable authorities that man can lead a healthier life purely on a plant-based diet, establishing this claim by scientific evidence and statistical data – provided the diet is a well-balanced mixture of vegetables, fruit, nuts, cereals and lentils, etc.

Normally, vegetarians add dairy products to the above list, including milk, butter, cheese and sometimes eggs. They are called 'lacto-ovo-vegetarians'. Those who abstain from dairy or any other kind of animal products are called 'vegans'. For meat-eaters, the writer has taken the liberty of poetic licence by coining the word 'meatarians' for lack of any other single word in English. It has always been taken for granted that man is in any case a meat-eater and, therefore, the word 'carnivore' has become solely associated with animal meat-eaters.

It is an established fact now that meat, with all its ingrained saturated fat, is not an ideal diet. Medical evidence shows that cholesterol is produced much more by animal fats than by polyunsaturated vegetable oils. Let us try to understand in simple words why animal fats are harmful for our health. The function of the heart is to pump about 5,000 gallons of blood every twenty-four hours. With every beat of the heart all the arteries in the body, especially the large ones, shrink and expand (pulsate) to circulate the blood. Too much fat causes swellings in the layers (plaques) of the smaller vessels and makes the arteries less elastic. This interferes with the supply of blood to the various parts of the body. In order to keep the flow of blood normal through the swollen arteries, the heart has to work so much harder and goes on becoming weaker. All the diseases associated with the circulation of the blood and the coronary arteries are generally called 'rich man's diseases' because rich people eat more fatty and richer food. Diseases such as the following are more common in wealthy countries than in the poor: high blood pressure, angina or thromboids in the coronary vessels of the heart, circulatory disturbances in the legs, diabetes, gout and cerebral haemorrhage in the brain.

The major controversy used to be over sources of protein, as only meat was considered to be the first class source of it, containing all the ten essential amino-acids. In fact, research has shown that by combining the various types of non-meat foods – such as pulses, beans, cereals, lentils, all kinds of vegetables, fruits and nuts – in a suitable balance and rotation, all the essential amino-acids can be ingested. Many of the old concepts of protein have now been found to be fallacious. For example, the idea that meat contains 'first-class' and vegetables 'second-class' protein has been proved to be wrong. Protein should be measured in terms of essential amino-acids which are of ten kinds. It is true that no one item of plant food contains all ten kinds of amino-acids; that is why dieticians recommend a mixture of plant-foods so that jointly they would make up for each other's deficiencies and produce the required balance of protein. For that matter, even meat on its own does not contain all the essential nutrients. Examples will be given later of people who live on animal products alone and, as a result, are suffering from degenerative diseases.

THE IMPORTANCE OF VITAMINS

In order to appreciate fully the importance of vitamins, especially of Vitamin B, one has to study their function in the body. It will not be easy for a layman to understand the medical terms in which it is generally explained by scientists. Still it is hoped that he would be able to get a general idea from the following explanation:

Enzymes are organic substances in a body, formed by living cells. They are capable of effecting a chemical change (by catalytic action) in other bodies without undergoing any change in themselves. The Vitamin B coenzymes function in the enzyme systems which transfer certain groups between molecules. The very life of the molecules depends on the Vitamin B enzymes.

In terms of their functions, vitamins are distinct from carbohydrates and proteins. Owing to the insufficiency of data available so far, medical opinion is not unanimous on various dietetic matters. It is, however, agreed that an inadequate supply of any one vitamin may lead to a condition known as 'hypovitaminosis' which affects the physiological functions of the body and hampers its growth. A deficiency of vitamins due to diet is called 'Primary' deficiency and it is a known fact that some of the harmful effects of this type of deficiency cannot be put right.

Until a few years ago, it was generally believed that the only dependable source of Vitamin B was animal flesh. However, it has now been discovered that all the different kinds of Vitamin B, as well as protein, minerals, carbohydrates and fats which the human body needs, are also found in plant foods. For example, yeast, bran (separated husks of grain) and germs of cereals and pulses contain them in the form of thiamine, riboflavin, niacin, etc. The only kind of Vitamin B for which the major source is meat is B12. However, although animal products are the major source of it, it is not exclusively the only source. An appreciable amount of B12 is contained in yeast, soya beans, wheatgerm, eggs and in sea-kelp and spirulina (types of algae or seaweed) and can be bought in powdered form. It is significant to know that the recommended daily dose of it is so small – only 3 to 5 micrograms – that it could easily be obtained from non-meat sources.

Careful studies have shown that the most likely deficiencies of Vitamin B12 and iron are not found even in strict vegans who do not eat any kind of animal products. The incidence of pernicious anaemia is no more prevalent among them than among meatarians. On the contrary, statistics show that meatarians suffer more from Vitamin B12 deficiency than vegetarians and vegans. It is not only the lack of vitamins that causes such illnesses – there are other nutritional deficiencies too which could cause them and prevent the body from utilising the vitamins, especially B12, such as the failure of the lower part of the intestinal tract (ileum) to absorb it. Normally, vegans and vegetarians enjoy long and healthier lives. Even if it is true that meat-abstinence causes deficiency of Vitamin B12, it could always be augmented by other supplements – as happens in other cases of deficiencies. Many vegan foods (such as yeast extracts) are supplemented with B12. The killing of animals to obtain Vitamin B12 or other nutrients is not the only remedy.

It is paradoxical that man consumes the flesh of those animals which are vegetarians themselves, such as cows, sheep and goats, to obtain vitamins in general and B12 in particular. If B12 is obtainable only from meat, where do these animals, who do not eat flesh, get their supply of Vitamin B12? Elephants develop the strongest physique and live longer than most animals by deriving their nutrients and vitamins from a kind of grass which is the poorest of all grasses. The life-expectancy of elephants is 60 years. It is not generally known to lay-people that there are certain kinds of vitamins, such as C, A, E and K which are non-existent in meat but can be obtained from vegetables or dairy products. The best source of Vitamin D is God's gift to His creation – the sun's rays.

The additional advantage of vegetarian food is that plant-protein contains much lower levels of cholesterol which is implicated in various arterial and heart diseases. As early as 1961 a medical survey in America, published in *The Journal of the American Medical Association*, revealed that:

" ... a vegetarian diet can prevent 90 per cent of our thrombo-embolic disease and 97 per cent of our coronary occlusions."

The current hedonistic philosophy in the rich West and America is guided by the doctrine that pleasure is the chief good, as William Gilmore puts it:

"Eat, drink and be merry, for tomorrow we die."

The choice of food is no longer dictated by the chemistry of our bodies, but by the taste of our tongues – which more often than not is perverted. This trend of faddishness for unnatural food is costing man, especially in the opulent West, much more than is printed on the menus of candle-lit restaurants – the real price he pays is in the currency of his health.

Too many deaths in these countries are premature and are caused mostly by unnatural and bizarre carnivorousness. The 'hidden persuaders' engaged by the multi-million pound international meat business have succeeded in changing man into an omnivore. The chemico-hormones on which animals and birds are fed in some modern intensive factory farms carry various kinds of poisons. Even fish in rivers and lakes are no longer safe. Statistics show that in the United Kingdom, for example, about 80 per cent of food-poisoning cases are caused by meat. Both physical and nervous diseases, such as coronary thrombosis, blood-pressure, diabetes, cancer and various other ailments, are on the increase. Excessive consumption of red meat and some types of char-grilled meat has been associated with some particular cancers. According to the medical science dealing with children's health (paediatrics), our modern unnatural diet is having still greater adverse effect on the younger generations.

It would be wrong to generalise the effect of diet alone on health and the longevity of life from individual cases. One does occasionally come across individuals who have been eating meat, smoking and playing ducks and drakes with the hygienic principles of health all their lives and still manage to live long and uninfectious lives. On the other hand, there are some lacto-ovo-vegetarians and vegans who are not sound in body. In spite of the fact that food is the most material factor, there are various other factors too which influence one's health – such as genetic heredity and variations, salubrity of the environment, mental disposition, and general lifestyle, etc. It is only from an empiric study, based on long-term observation and experiment of a class of people, that logical inferences can be drawn.

Take for example the Masais of East Africa among whom the writer has lived for many years. Their diet is blood, milk and meat. Or the Eskimos who live mostly on meat and fish. It is an anthropological fact that both these people are now suffering from an increase in various degenerative diseases. As opposed to that, there are vegetarian races who live much longer and healthier lives. The Hunzakuts of Kashmir are known to be one of the healthiest people on earth with a naturally long span of life. Their diet is mainly vegetarian. The writer has personally met some Hunzakuts and was greatly impressed by the simplicity of their taste and lifestyle. It is not that the climate of Kashmir is the only reason. The climate of the Andes in South America is no better than the rest of that part of the world. Not so long ago an Andean tribe was discovered in an outlandish part of the Andes which had so far escaped contact with our so-called civilised world. It was discovered that in one of their villages with a population of 400, there were many over the age of 100 years, 38 over the age of 75 and one over 121 years. Their medical examination showed that only two old people had any signs of heart disease. The diet of these people consists basically of plants, herbs, and wild fruit.[2]

THE ANATOMY OF MAN

The secret of health lies in eating what the chemistry of the body needs and for which its anatomy is structured. All the anatomical evidence of the human body shows that the organs and limbs of man have not been designed to obtain food by predacity. He has no claws to tear the prey with; the flimsy little nails he has are not retractable. His teeth are non canine and he has no fangs and cutters; they are not sharp and strong enough to gnaw, crush bones or to flay a carcass. The munching movement of his jaws is like that of the herbivorous animals. Unarmed, he cannot fight tooth and nail even a wild cat. The fact that he cannot perform such functions without the aid of tools confirms the point that God did not design his body to kill for food, otherwise He would have equipped it with tools as He did the other beasts of prey. Even his internal organs and whole digestive system is not designed for a fleshy diet. His stomach does not secrete enough hydrochloric acid to liquate bones and other indigestibles, as the stomachs of all carnivorous animals do. Since the excreta of carnivores is much fouler and noxious, nature has provided them with much shorter alimentary canals for rapid emptying of the bowels after they have eaten flesh, so that it does not remain in the body longer than necessary; the canals of herbivores are longer. Man's digestive system in this section also follows more closely to the pattern of herbivores. Uric acid in the body has a poisonous effect and causes various kinds of diseases. Human kidneys cannot convert the uric acid into *gloxyl urea*, as do the kidneys of all carnivores.

Whatever way you look at it, it becomes obvious that man belongs to the herbivorous order of species. The nearest animals to man, biologically, are the genera of anthropoid apes. Everything anatomical between them and man is almost the same, except that they are arboreal (living in trees) while man is terrestrial (living on the ground). The differences of intellectual and spiritual capacities do not warrant a discussion, as we are dealing here with physical food and not with mental or spiritual pabulum. The blood of apes is essentially identical to that of man. The menstrual cycle in chimpanzees and gorillas has the same phases as in human females. The gestation period (between conception and birth) of nine months is the same. The organ which is attached to the foetus by the umbilical cord and falls out after birth (placenta) is alike. In spite of all these anatomical and biological similarities, almost all apes have remained basically vegetarian, without suffering from deficiencies of any kind of vitamins including B12, while man has become a meatarian. Nobody knows exactly at what stage of evolution this change occurred in man, because all the anthropological evidence shows that man started life on Earth as a herbivore. It should not go unnoticed that we in our time are witnessing another phase in human evolution. Man is changing fast into an omnivore, i.e. he has started eating anything and everything that is on offer.

THE ECONOMICS OF FOOD

The current use of agricultural land for food-animals does not make any economic sense. It is proving to be a miscomputation as well as amoral. There are highly specialised people in this field who are much better qualified than the writer to advise on this subject. However the writer looks at this problem more from moral and ethical points of view than the mundane pros and cons of the modern agricultural scenario. But, to give the devil his due, the subject has to be discussed from the earthly point of view in the light of the current unfortunate trend in the developing countries to follow the Western plough and to warn them of the disaster they are heading for by depleting their exhaustible natural resources, irrespective of economic as well as ecological exigencies. The spade-husbandmen in the developing countries are too busy working and scraping their meagre fare, as best they can, to know what is happening in the rest of the world. For example, it never crosses their minds that, if the present agrarian outrage is allowed to continue, sooner or later the world will have to become vegetarian by force. Perhaps the following facts and figures will make them think twice before they allow themselves to fall into the same trap as the short-sighted Western farmers have fallen.

At present approximately one quarter of the world's total land area is being used for grazing livestock and 30% or more of the global cereal harvest and most of its soya harvest is fed to farm animals, while millions of human beings go hungry or starve to death. If the available land and all its resources were to be utilised for sensible agriculture, it could feed far more mouths than the present human population of the world. We need 100 acres of fertile land to pasture enough food animals to feed 20 people. The same 100 acres could produce enough maize to feed 100 people; or wheat to feed 240 people; or beans to feed 610 people. In Great Britain, for example, we consume about 850 million animals every year. To feed these animals we import cereals from countries where the general populace is suffering from malnutrition and wasting diseases.

Famines in various parts of Africa should be read by economists as the ominous writing on the wall. There are various reasons for such famines, but the root of this sorry plight is the short-sighted policy of the developed countries to tempt the under-developed regions of the world to grow cash-crops for export, instead of their indigenous food. Most of these cash-crops are seeds and cereals for livestock. If a small country such as Britain were to utilise all its land for growing human food instead of herbage for animals, it would be able to feed more than four times its present population of about 56 million people.

This is what a prominent writer on this subject, Jon Wynne-Tyson, has to say about the current state of affairs:

> "... think for a moment what the habit of meat-eating involves in terms of the world's food supplies ... . About four-fifths of the world's agricultural land is used for feeding animals, and only about one-fifth for feeding man directly. This fact, shocking in its implications, has been examined by nutritionists Frank Wokes (editor-in-chief of *Plant Foods for Human Nutrition* and chairman of the Plant Foods Research Trust) and Cyril Vesey (University Department of Clinical Neurology, London) in their paper *'Land, Food and the People'*, Part One of the series "*Perspectives in Nutrition*":

> "At the beginning of this decade there were about 35 hundred million people in the world ... . The rich Western nations, occupying half of the world's agricultural land, amounted to only about two-sevenths of the world's population; whereas the poor, mainly Eastern, occupying the other half of the world's agricultural land, amounted to about

five-sevenths. Moreover, the poor Eastern people live mainly in the tropics where the yields of crops are often less than a quarter of those in the Western countries. Multiplying the yields factor of about 4 by the population density factor of about 2A we get a differential of about 10 between the average food crop production of the average Westerner and that of the average Easterner. The average Westerner does not, of course, eat 10 times but only 1A times as much food as the average Easterner. But he consumes much more animal food, about five times as much animal protein and animal calories as the Easterner. He is able to do this only because he has two-and-a-half times as much agricultural land on which to produce his food, and this on the average is several times more fertile. But because the people in Western countries consume much more animal food, he even needs to import materials to feed his animals as well as himself.

"When we consider the work and cost and wastage that goes into stock-breeding in order that the world's affluent minority can indulge in so unnecessary a luxury, the sheer extravagance and foolishness of it all is staggering. We read in our newspapers about the starving and under-fed millions, and all the time we are feeding to meat-producing animals the very crops that could more than eradicate world food shortage; also, we are importing from starving nations large quantities of grain and other foods that are then fed to our animals instead of to the populations who produce them.

"In our greed to profit from the under-developed world, we have already gone to great lengths to popularise meat-eating among nations whose diet was previously largely or wholly meat-excluding.

"Most of the fertile land devoted to cattle – which eat cereals, root and green crops and various seeds for improved milk production – could show a much quicker and more economical return if used for crops suitable for direct feeding to human beings...

> "It is to our shame that such revelations are far from new. Much further back Sir John Russell, FRS, and others before him, made similar estimates showing incontrovertibly that plant foods, if fed directly to man rather than after processing through animals, can increase the yield per acre by up to ten-fold. As an example, soya beans yield seven times as much amino-acid per acre as milk production and eight times as much as egg production.
>
> "Plant foods create protein from water, carbon dioxide and nitrogen, which is why they are the primary source of protein today … . This above all is why governments, economists, industrialists and international welfare organisations have begun to realise that the sooner the cow, the chicken and other victims of our prodigal way of life are replaced by food made from plant proteins the better for the world at large."[3]

All this absurd extravagance and waste is being perpetuated in spite of modern scientific evidence that the human body can derive all its nourishment from a fibrous diet exclusive of meat and other animal products. Almost all kinds of edible nuts – such as peanuts, walnuts, almonds, cashew-nuts, Brazil nuts – give more calories, protein and vitamins pound for pound than meat, in addition to having many other advantages over meat. The argument that nuts and fruit work out more expensive than meat for a family of average means is just a lame excuse. There is no part of the world where meat is cheaper. In these days of inter-continental means of transport, all kinds of vegetables, fruits and nuts are available in places where they cannot be grown. The reason why fruit and nuts are comparatively dearer is because they are not grown in enough quantities. Why? Because they have not yet become regular items of the daily diet. The law of supply and demand does not justify their cultivation other than on purely economic grounds. The writer (during his travels by car in the East, mainly through Islamic countries, covering about 70,000 kilometres over a period of about three years) often passed through miles and miles of hilly country where various kinds of fruit and nuts could easily be grown. The only signs of life which he and his wife used to see in such expanses of virgin hills were a few rambling flocks of sheep and goats.

Horticulture of fruit and nuts has many positive advantages over the breeding of food-animals. Once a tree has taken root, it does not need much attention, unlike livestock which demand constant daily chores as well as the cost of fodder. Dried fruit and nuts do not need any contrivances such as refrigerators to keep them longer or chemical additives to preserve them as meat does. There is little danger of their getting putrefied and becoming a health hazard, as meat sometimes does with its poisonous chemicals. Without doubt they are much cheaper to grow and would be much cheaper to buy, once the increase in demand starts encouraging the supply.

Soya beans require one acre of land to produce as much nutrition as milk would through cows using five or six acres. There is no animal or plant food which can beat the humble soya bean in nutritional value. It contains Vitamin A, B_1, and B_2, has a high calorie count, iron, calcium, phosphorous, 23 per cent unsaturated fat, and a high content of the amino-acid lysine, but it is low carbohydrate and has almost no starch. Milk, for which cows are subjected to great physical and emotional cruelties, contains no iron. The cycle of their yearly pregnancies has to be kept uninterrupted for the regular supply of milk. Calves are separated from their mothers as early as possible and are fed on such stimulative foods for rapid growth as to make them ready for their own cycle of pregnancies before reaching the age of two years.

Just to take a few more examples: a banana gives as much energy as the same weight of beef. Recent experiments have succeeded in extracting protein and fat from leaves – about 20 per cent protein and about 25 per cent unsaturated fat. In order to grow 3 million calories through animal products, 20 acres of grazing land is needed; while walnut trees on only one acre would produce the same amount of calories. The following chart shows the comparative properties of almonds and beef:

COMPARATIVE FOOD-VALUES OF BEEF AND ALMONDS

100 grams (5.5 ounces)	Calories	Protein	Energy KCAL	Value KJ	Carbo Hydrates	Calcium	Fat	Water Content
Lean Beef Steak	242	14.8%	313%	1,311%	0%	8mg	28.2%	59%
Almonds	580	20.5%	580%	2,430%	4.3%	247mg	53.5%	5%

This book is not meant to be a dietary manual. Those interested in the subject should get more authentic information from the books listed in Reference No. 4 at the end of the Chapter. The above Chart has been prepared by the writer from the same books.[4]

The moral and ethical principles in the issue are even more complicated than the biological aspects of it. If and when people are convinced that adequate sources of nutrients other than meat are available, it should not be difficult to make them change their bill of fare. However, deep-rooted immemorial traditions and some religious rituals are beyond the domain of reason. Right through the ages of cave-dwellers to the present jet-set day, the scenario of animal plight has been the same. All religions, including the most primitive disciplines, have been trying to strike a sensible and equitable balance in the relationship between man and animals, but man's greed and self-indulgence have always tempted him to circumvent those disciplines. During the early stages of man's spiritual evolution, even the voodoo priests and oracles tried to bring man into harmony with nature through animism, spiritualism and various other kinds of fetishism. Later on, the scriptural religions laid down elaborate laws to define the mutual rights and obligations of man and beast. While it is true that some religious disciplines have made the mistake of over-reaching themselves by imposing constraints and self-denial beyond the limits of practicability, the obverse of the coin these days presents a picture of opposite extremes in the shape of exploitation of animals by the disciples of Mammon.

As mentioned earlier, this chapter is meant to discuss the question of meat eating from the moral, and hence the religious, point of view. The point cannot be over-emphasised that apart from considerations of the physical and material advantages of a vegetarian diet over meat, the real concern of humane human beings should be their conscientious responsibilities towards the weaker species. The true altruistic spirit is that which engenders a sense of regard for others as a principle and not for the ulterior motive of gain or the expectation of advantage. It is time that civilised man should rise above "The Charters for HUMAN Rights" and start thinking in terms of Rights of ALL CREATURES. Morality within the circumscription of human species alone remains a misnomer unless it becomes all-embracing, including the tiniest of God's creatures in the comprehensive connotation of ecological morality. It is this all-absorbing kind of sublime morality to which all the divinely-inspired religions have been trying to edify man; while man has persistently been fighting shy of that edification in his self-indulgent gratification of fleshly pleasures and appetites.

There is no doubt that both hygienic and economic factors are in favour of a vegetarian diet, but the issue goes beyond these mundane considerations. Our moral responsibility toward the welfare of the rest of the species demands that we employ all our scientific knowledge to acquiring as much of our nutrients as possible from sources other than the flesh of those animals whom God has created and who are at our mercy. Let us see how some of our religions have endeavoured to solve this moral problem.

CONFUCIANISM

Classical Confucianism does not throw any light on the question of meat-eating. The code of morality taught by Confucius(s), on which the Chinese, Korean and Japanese cultures were developed and which ultimately became the State religion of China, does not concern itself directly with the welfare of animals. The Analects (551-479 B.C.), however, mention some anecdotes about Confucius(s) which depict him as a man of high moral principles (*chun-*

tzu) who would kill animals only if necessary, but would not take undue advantage of them. For example, he caught fish by hook and bait and did not use a net, nor did he hunt a roosting bird.[5] Another anecdote throws a different light on his character. Once, his stables were burnt down. On hearing the news, his only concern was to know if any human beings were hurt. He was not interested in knowing about the fate of the horses.[6]

However, such stories are often misleading and should not be taken seriously, especially when one is seeking an insight into the character of such a great and highly moral personality as Confucius[(s)] who gave the world a great religion. We know, for example, that he gave the people of those olden days a new concept of heaven (*Tien-li*) which accommodated not only human beings but also animals and plants.

There is one incident recorded and repeatedly discussed in Confucian literature which throws light on the psychology of meat-eaters and which could be applied even in the modern context. People buy their meat at butchers' shops without giving it a thought that the neatly wrapped-up joints were once parts of the body of an animal which would still be alive and kicking but for the butcher's knife. The story runs as follows:

A king once saw a man leading an ox to the altar and ordered him to release it. The man remonstrated, explaining that the slaughter of the ox was by way of a sacrifice. The king did not want to interfere with the ritual of a sacrifice but, at the same time, he was moved with pity for the ox. He, therefore, ordered the man to replace the ox with a sheep.

The great Confucian sage, Mencius (*Meng-Tzu*)[7] while discussing the incident with the king analysed his behaviour in these words: "Your conduct was an artifice of benevolence. You saw the ox and had not seen the sheep. So is the superior man affected towards animals that, having seen them alive, he cannot bear to see them die; having heard their dying cries, he cannot bear to eat their flesh."[8] One wonders how many people would still relish their Sunday joints if they ever happened to watch the slaughtering of animals in an abattoir.

The spiritual and cultural influence of Confucianism and Neo-Confucianism notwithstanding, most of East Asia has ended up as heterodox in the choice of food in the real sense of omnivorousness. Vegetarianism as a creed has no place in their cuisine. Although their overall meat consumption is far lower than in the West, it is rapidly increasing. It is believed by some that the Japanese used to be vegetarians until some 250 years ago.

HINDUISM, JAINISM AND BUDDHISM

The Sanskrit word 'Veda' means knowledge. The Vedas are the most ancient sacred literature of Hindus (cir. 1500 to 1000 B.C.), comprising more than one hundred books, which have been collected in four Vedas, namely: Rig Veda, Yajur Veda, Sama Veda, and Atharva Veda. They advocate vegetarianism throughout their teachings. Based on such teachings, the *Manu Samhita*, which is the ancient Indian code of law, states:

> "Meat can never be obtained without injury to living creatures, and injury to sentient beings is detrimental to the attainment of heavenly bliss; let him [man] therefore shun the use of meat." In another section, it warns: "Having well considered the disgusting origin of flesh and the cruelty of slaying of corporeal beings, let him entirely abstain from eating flesh." It goes on to say "One whose flesh I eat will eat my flesh in the next life." Similarly, the *Annu Shasen Perva Mahabharat* gives the verdict: "Undoubtedly all those human beings who prefer meat to several other forms of food are like vultures." According to the Vedas, all living beings possess a soul and, hence, they all are equal in that sense, although they have different bodies and different levels of intelligence.

It is generally believed that Hindus have been vegetarians from the beginning. Their early records, however, put some doubt on this claim. There is some evidence that they used to fish and hunt, and also killed domestic animals for food.[9] Many historical records could be quoted, but the following few examples would suffice here:

> "Formerly, in the kitchen of the beloved of gods, King Priyadarsin [Emperor Asoka, 274-232 B.C.], a hundred thousand animals were killed every day for the sake of curry. But now after Asoka had embraced Buddhism when this *Dharma-script* [the Buddhist decree or custom] is written, only three animals are killed ...".[10]

It must, however be understood that the conduct of a lay person such as the Emperor Asoka should not be taken as an exemplification of the Hindu doctrine. What used to happen in his court is just a reflection on the social life of that period.

A Brahmin belongs to the highest sacerdotal or priestly caste of the Hindu society which is divided into four hereditary hierarchical grades. According to an anecdote recorded in the *Encyclopaedia of Buddhism*, a rabbit once coming upon a hungry Brahmin, lighted a fire and jumped into it to be roasted so that the Brahmin could eat him.[11] The fact that, according to the story, the hungry Brahmin was the god Indra who had appeared to the rabbit in the guise of a Brahmin makes no difference to the inference that the Brahmins in those days did eat rabbits.

The ancient Vedic literature repeatedly narrates stories on the theme of mutual feelings of sacrifice between man and animals, even to the point of the ultimate sacrifice of life for each other. Such stories are not meant to be fairy tales for children. They are taken in the literal sense by millions of Hindus, even these days, and have been influencing the attitudes of the Hindu laity towards animals for about the last three thousand years. The following story, for example, is meant to transfuse a sense of the doctrine of re-birth:

A Brahmin was once about to kill a goat as a sacrifice when the goat started laughing and crying alternately. When asked why, the goat explained: "I was laughing out of happiness because this time I shall be reborn as a human being, after having passed through 500 rebirths as a goat; I was crying out of pity for you because the same is going to happen to you as happened with me. I was originally condemned from Brahminhood to 500 lives as a goat for sacrificing a goat. If you kill me, you too shall be condemned to a similar fate." The story has a happy ending: the Brahmin did not kill the goat and continued to live as a human being, while the goat was struck by lightning and was reborn as a human.[12]

It was only at a later stage, perhaps under the influence of Jainism and Buddhism, that meat-eating became sacrilegious for Hindus. Vegetarianism in the West is practised mostly out of compassion for animals. The Hindu abstinence from meat, however, is based on the pantheistic philosophy or wisdom (*Vedanta*) leading to non-violence and re-birth. The doctrine of non-violence (*ahimsa*) cannot be explained better than in the following words of *Acaranga Sutra*:

> "Injurious activities inspired by self-interest lead to evil and darkness. This is what is called bondage, delusion, death, and hell. To do harm to others is to do harm to oneself. Thou art he whom thou intendest to kill ...! Thou art he whom thou intendest to tyrannize! We corrupt ourselves as soon as we intend to corrupt others."[13]

The doctrine of rebirth is very relevant to the subject of animals' welfare in general and meat-eating in particular. We are not concerned here with the theological intricacies of this doctrine. Nevertheless, it must be appreciated that it has played a significant role in influencing the behaviour towards animals of millions of people throughout the various parts of the sub-continent of India as well as in East, South and Central Asia. The moral aspect of this influence can be appreciated only after getting some idea of the theological fundamentals on which the concept of reincarnation, and hence rebirth, is based, which can be summarised as follows:

a. All the 'animals' and the so-called 'inanimate' beings (*sat*) pass through a continuous succession of changes. In the case of the 'inanimate' beings (*ajiva*), the changes take place through metamorphoses, i.e. changes of form or condition by natural development; in the case of human and other 'animate' beings (*jiva*), the process of change is through metempsychoses, i.e. the transmigration of soul at death into a new body belonging to the same or a different species.
b. The highest grade in the hierarchy of the 'animate' beings is that of humans; next comes the grade of animals; and so on.
c. The inherent propensity of each 'animate' is to try to rise to a higher status in each incarnation, by gaining merit through good deeds, with the proviso that each individual creature is responsible for its salvation through its deeds or *Karma*.
d. Some succeed in improving their lot, while others get demoted by way of punishment for bad deeds. The vilest of such deeds is considered to be violence, harm or injury (*hims*) in any form.
e. The final haven of rest, after a long struggle of 'action' (*karma*) and successive states of flux (*samsara*), is the state of 'inaction' – a state of bliss, purity and freedom, called *Mukt, Moksha* or *Nirvana.*

Admittedly, the above is a feeble attempt at the simplification of very elaborate concepts of theology but, hopefully, it will serve to make a few relevant points.

To give credence to the concept that an animal could have been one's close relative in the previous incarnation or that one could become an animal in the next incarnation is daunting enough to inhibit the killing and eating of animals. How could one swallow the flesh of an animal who, according to the *Lankavatara Sutra*, could have been anyone of the following:

> "In the long course of '*samsara*' (successive incarnations), there is not one among living beings with form who has not been mother, father, brother, sister, son, daughter, or some other relative. Being connected

with the process of [repeated] births, one is kin to all wild and domestic animals, birds, and beings born from the womb."

According to the *Brahmajala Sutra* of the Buddhists:

" ... all the living beings of the six *gati* [categories of beings] are our parents; and if we kill them, we kill our parents and also our former bodies ...".[14]

As mentioned before, some believe that the emphasis on vegetarianism in Hindu thought came from Jainism and Buddhism. Jainism is a reform movement within the spectrum of Hinduism. The origin of this movement, as of Buddhism, can be traced back to the late 6th or early 5th century B.C. Both believe in vegetarianism; strongly condemn the Hindu practice of animal sacrifice; reject quite a few of the dogmas associated with Vedas; and both deny the existence of a personal and a creative God.

Jainism is claimed to have been started by some pre-historic Jaina monks, but the one who has been recorded in history as the founder is called Rusabhdev. However Vardhamana Mahavira (599-527 B.C.) is also given a very prominent place by historians. He was the 24th *Tirthankara* in the line of succession. Like the Gautama Buddha, he also came from a princely family. The founder of Buddhism was Buddha (the wise sage) Gautama Sidhartha or Sakya Sinha or Muni (563-483 B.C.).

Although Jains are still counted as Hindus, they have earned for themselves a distinct identity as a religion within a religion. Originally, in line with the Hindu prejudice against crossing the waters, they too had remained confined within the shores of India, but now they have settled in many parts of the world. In spite of being less than one per cent (about 4/5 million), they wield a great influence on overall Hindu thought. They are mostly centred in Ahmedabad, the famous city of India where Mahatma Gandhi spent twelve years of his life and became greatly influenced by Jainism.

Like the Confucians, Jains too believe that all creatures are equal and possess a soul. Their doctrines, such as non-injury to animals in the general sense of *Ahimsa*, and successive rebirths, are no doubt very benedictory to animal welfare. However, some of their idealistic interpretations are perhaps too far stretched and difficult to practise. Let us take a few examples:

For fear of killing germs and insects, Jains are not supposed to eat root vegetables such as potatoes, or to pulp and grind grains. One of the five tenets of *Ahimsa* is that one should eat only during day-time, before sunset. From a health point of view it is a very wise proposition. Even modern dieticians recommend that it is not healthy to retire for the night on a heavy stomach. However, the reason given in the religious sources of this tenet is that, after dark, there is a greater possibility of insects in the air getting in the mouth along with the morsels of food.[15] One should not travel far from home lest one should cause harm to 'beings' in an unfamiliar place.[16] Worms and insects in the soil get injured by digging or ploughing, therefore farming is considered as one of the contra-ahimsa occupations.[17] One Jain sect, called the Digamaras, denounces even activities such as bathing, use of fire, wearing of clothes, farming *etcetera*, for fear of hurting the creatures in air, water or earth.[18]

The early Buddhists, in general, were more liberal than the Jains in meat-eating, but gradually vegetarianism became the norm. Many Buddhist sects these days are staunch vegetarians although other Buddhists take the view that one should eat what one is offered, even if it includes meat. Buddhists in south-east Asia are often fish-eaters too. Some Buddhist teachings have gone to the opposite extremes of non-violence against animals by recommending that human beings should offer their bodies to the animals as food. One such text reads as follows:

> "One should be willing to forsake one's entire body, one's flesh, hands and feet as an offering to starving tigers, wolves, lions and hungry ghosts."[19]

Many of the stringently moral and ethical standards, as laid down in the above disciplines of Jainism and Buddhism, were beyond measure for an average person. It was therefore, right from the beginning, found necessary to chalk out two separate codes of practice – one for the layman (*anuvrata*); and one for the monks (*dhikhu or mahavrata*). The monks are to observe the laws of *Ahimsa* to the letter while the laity is allowed some leeway in matters of detail. The monks, for example, are to confine themselves in their monasteries during the monsoon season, because the insects and worms which come out of their holes in the rain could get crushed under their feet.[20] They are to be abstemious not only in food, which would naturally be vegetarian, but also should suppress all fleshly appetites including sex.[21]

Notwithstanding all this priestly code, the Buddhist monks (*Blama*) living in the bleak Tibetan and Mongolian mountains eat meat, as they say, to survive. Their excuse that meat is a necessity for them is belied by the presence of the Zanskar Buddhists amongst them in the same mountains who are strict vegetarians. However, the meat-eating Buddhists derive some consolation from the fact that they do not hunt or kill the animals themselves – they engage others to do it for them.

It is a very sad fact that dogmatism invariably ends up in defeating the very purpose for which the related doctrine was originally laid down. If the purpose of *Ahimsa* (non-injury) is to spare all living creatures any pain and suffering, then some believe the Jains are guilty of neglecting the spirit of that principle. Basing their code of practice on the theory that deeds (*Karma*) and suffering follow the natural course of 'cause and effect', they may allow sick and injured animals to die a lingering death instead of putting an end to their suffering by 'mercy-killing'. Once Mahatma Gandhi allowed a suffering calf to be killed by euthanasia and was strongly criticised by the Jains.

It must be mentioned here that the writer has always believed in the intrinsic and altruistic philosophies based on the original teachings of the Jain, Buddhist and Hindu prophets (may God bless all of them). The above criticism is not against these religions as such; it is meant to point out the greatest of all priestly weaknesses, namely to play God in trying to uplift man above the laws of nature and put so much stress on his physical capabilities that, instead of bending, he breaks, or opts for the easy way out and tells the priests to 'go to hell'.

It seems very appropriate to end this section of the book with a few words of wisdom from a Buddha who is amongst us, living as an exile in India – His Holiness Tenzin Gyatso the fourteenth Dalai Lama:

> "Even the lowest insect strives for protection against dangers that threaten its life. Just as each one of us wants happiness and fears pain, just as each one of us wants to live and not to die, so do all other creatures."[22]

CHRISTIANITY

There is very little to be said about Christianity in respect of vegetarianism or meatarianism. Jesus Christ[(s)] has not been recorded as saying anything definitive on this subject, and his silence is taken by Christians as leaving the decision on diet to individual choice.

Jesus[(s)], personally, has been mentioned in the Gospels (*Injīl*) about sixteen times as eating meat. However, some Biblical scholars take the view that the Greek word translated into the English Bible as 'meat' actually means 'food' and not necessarily the flesh of an animal. Even in the Old Testament the word 'meat' has often been used in the sense of food in general, which includes vegetables, fruit and cereals. In the Third Book of Moses[23] the word 'meat' is used for flour. Again, after explaining how to offer bullocks, sheep and fowls, it reads:

> "And when any will offer a meat offering unto the Lord, his offering shall be of fine flour … ."[24]

Modern English also uses the word 'meat' as a figure of speech for any kind of solid food in the form of flesh as well as the edible parts of vegetables, fruits and nuts. To say 'before or after meat' used to mean 'before or after a meal'. Although there is no conclusive historical evidence for it, it is believed by some that Jesus[(s)] was born in a Jewish community called Essenes who used to lead a monastic type life and were vegetarians. Basing their argument on that, some Christians have started believing that Jesus[(s)] himself was a vegetarian. There are still many Essenes living in Israel these days and they are vegetarians. It is estimated that about 4 – 12 per cent of Israelis are vegetarian. According to the *Essene Gospel of Peace*, which is based on the original Aramaic text, Jesus [(s)] is recorded to have said:

> "... For I tell you truly, he who kills, kills himself, and who so eats the flesh of slain beasts, eats the body of death."

The Essenes claim that their version of the Bible is the most authentic one, free from the later alterations and revisions. For example, according to their records, the parents of Jesus[(s)], Joseph and Mary, did not sacrifice a lamb during the feast of Passover, that Jesus[(s)] himself replaced the Passover meal of the sacrificed lamb with 'bread and wine', and that John the Baptist (Yaḥyā)[(s)] and his disciples were vegetarian. The famous miracle of Jesus[(s)] when he fed about four thousand people with 'loaves and fish' was, according to their version, 'loaves and fruit' and not fish.

Some Christian theologians infer from verses 1-4 of St. John's Gospel that Christ[(s)] as the Logos of God (the Word of the Second Person of the Trinity) confirms the above inference. Those who give credence to this doctrine must also believe that Christ[(s)] could never have eaten the flesh of the same animals whom he created as a co-creator with God.[25] One wonders how much difference it would have made to the fate of all those millions of animals who are being killed for consumption in the Christian world, if it were to be established that Jesus[(s)] was a vegetarian. Some Christian theologians earnestly believe that, according to the Bible, God intended man to be vegetarian. In the words of the philosopher Karl Barth:

> "Whether or not we find it practicable or desirable, the diet assigned to man and beasts by God the Creator is vegetarian."[26]

JUDAISM AND ISLAM

The issue of vegetarianism versus meatarianism in the light of the Islamic concepts has to be discussed in conjunction with those of Judaism; not so much because of similarities between these two concepts, but because of dissimilarities. Both religions allow the use of animals for food in their respective scriptures, but the moral philosophy underlying this Covenant between God and them is not the same. In some cases the two concepts are discordantly incompatible with each other.

There is ample evidence in the Torah to support the claim of some Jews that God intended man to subsist on vegetables and abstain from meat. In the following verse, while describing the principles of those whose moral code of life is:

> "Let us eat and drink; for tomorrow we shall die", God mentions that such people derive their "joy and gladness" by "slaying oxen, and killing sheep, eating flesh, and drinking wine." Isaiah (the greatest of the Hebrew prophets, 740-701 B.C.) prophesies about such people: "And it was revealed in mine ears by the Lord of Hosts, surely this iniquity shall not be purged from you till ye die."[27] At the same time a ray of hope radiates in prophecies such as: "For, behold, I create new heavens and a new earth; and the former shall not be remembered nor come into mind. But be ye glad and rejoice for ever in that which I create ... The wolf and the lamb shall feed together, and the lion shall eat straw like the bullock: and dust shall be the serpent's meat. They shall not hurt nor destroy in all my holy mountain, saith the Lord."[28]

> "The wolf also shall dwell with the lamb, and the leopard shall lie down with the kid; and the calf and young lion and the fatling together; and a little child shall lead them."[29]

The real difficulty, however, in seeking guidancc from the Hebrew Bible for the practical conduct of life is that there are so many contradictory statements in it. There is so much confusion in the amalgam of Rabbinical appendages and the originally revealed version that one can find in it support for one's views ranging from sublime thought to the anomalous as well as to the ridiculous.

It must be pointed out here that Jewish vegetarians infer from verses 29 and 30, Chapter 1, of Genesis that the Hebrew Bible does not permit food based on meat or any other kind of animal product. They interpret these verses as specifically suggesting a vegan diet. They read as follows:

> "And God said, Behold, I have given you every herb bearing seed, which is upon the face of all the earth, and every tree in which is the fruit of a tree yielding seed; to you it shall be for meat ... and I have given every green herb for meat ... [i.e. as food]."

Jewish vegetarians, like many other Jewish scholars, believe that: "in the Noahtic laws, as in the consequent Hebrew laws given on Mount Sinai ..., permission granted to eat flesh ... was as a compromise"; that: "the sixth commandment, 'Thou shalt not kill' seals the general teachings relating to carnivorous habits"; that the phrase in Genesis: "To man and all creatures wherein is a living soul" proves that the prescribed diet of all living creatures, including human beings, is vegetarian.[30]

It has always been the general impression that the dietetic laws of both Judaism and Islam are the same. Even some Muslims have come to believe in this misconception. We are concerned here with the sanction of meat as food. This, however, cannot be explained or understood without reference to the historical and theological links between the two religions. Judaism has influenced the Muslim attitude so surreptitiously that most Muslims are not even conscious of it. The interactions between the two have influenced not only Muslim thought but also their general deportment. This susceptibility of Muslims is becoming increasingly notable in matters of *Ḥalāl* (lawful) and *Ḥarām* (unlawful) food; in the method of slaughter; and in the concept of animal sacrifice. This situation has stemmed from the impression among them that the Jewish dietetic laws are in accord with those of Islam in every detail. One of the reasons which has prompted such misconceptions is the Islamic concurrence with some of the theologies of the previous revealed religions in general and Judaism in particular.

Muslims believe that Islam is not a new religion. Rather it is a continuation of all the previous monotheistic religions whose teachings it incorporates *mutatis mutandis*. The Qur'ān , for example acknowledges all the Biblical prophets as the true Messengers of God and goes further by vindicating their character from the imperfections which the Old Testament has ascribed to some of them. This kind of theological affinity with Judaism was based on monotheism – a link which is still strong and valid.

In the verse below the Qur'ān puts a formal proposal for an alliance between all the monotheistic religions, which has been rendered into a free translation by the late Mawlānā Abū'l Kalām Āzād, the famous leader of the Indian National Congress and a great Muslim scholar, as follows:

> "*O Prophet [Muḥammad(s)]! say to the Jews and the Christians: 'O people of the Book! Let us not wrangle over what may be regarded as controversial subjects. Let us at least agree on that which is recognised alike by you and by us, i.e. that we worship none but God and associate nothing with Him, and take not each other as Lord to the exclusion of God...*'" (Qur'ān 3:64)[31]

The Holy Prophet Muḥammad(s) sent letters containing the text of this verse to the Heads of various kingdoms, such as Heracleus, in 627 A.C. A copy of this letter, sent to Muqawqis – the Pharaoh of Egypt, was later discovered and found to be a verbatim copy of the version as recorded in the book of *Ḥadīth*, *Ṣaḥīḥ* of Bukhārī.[32]

It was in the same spirit of promoting goodwill and social intercourse among the monotheistic religions that the Qur'ān declared:

> "*This day [all] good and pure things have been made lawful for you, and the food of the heritors of previous Scriptures is lawful for you, and your food is lawful for them. And eligible for you are the chaste women both from among those who believe in Islam and those who are the heritors of the previous Scriptures, provided that you give them their due dowers – not committing fornication nor keeping them clandestinely as paramours.*" (Qur'ān 5:5)[33]

One feels sadly disappointed that historically the Jews did not respond favourably to this, and similar other overtures of Islam. It seems that their traditional attitudes towards mingling with other religions has often been guided by the following and similar commandments of the Old Testament:

> "And when the Lord thy God shall deliver them [the seven nations mentioned in the previous verse] before thee; thou shalt smite them, and utterly destroy them; thou shalt make no covenant with them, nor show mercy unto them. Neither shalt thou make marriages with them; thy daughter thou shalt not give unto his son, nor his daughter shalt thou take unto thy son."[34]

The Qur'ānic ethics of war are based on an integral body of laws which are beyond the scope of this book. Most fundamentally, Muslims are allowed to fight only defensive wars and are expressly forbidden to initiative the offensive.[35] Abū Bakr, the first Caliph after the death of the Holy Prophet Muḥammad[(s)] (632-634 A.C.) addressed the Muslim army at a place outside Madina, called Jurf, before sending them off for the battle of Mu'tah. Among the ten instructions he gave to the soldiers, the following throw some light on the Muslim ethics of war during a period when no mercy used to be shown to the defeated people. He ordered them not to mutilate anybody's limbs; not to kill old men, women or children; not to cut down fruit trees; not to slaughter animals except for food; and not to molest those living in monasteries. It is not only the residences of monks which Islam has declared as sacrosanct during a war. One of the reasons given in the Qur'ān which justifies a war is to protect the Jewish synagogues and the Christian churches – not only the Muslim mosques but all places of worship as well. It is noteworthy in the above instructions of the Caliph Abū Bakr that even the trees (environment) and the animals have been included in that list of protected things.[36]

The pivot on which this tripartite relationship between Judaism, Christianity and Islam oscillates is the personality of the Prophet Abraham[(s)], although Christians generally do not accord to him a status higher than that of one of the prophets. For the Jews he is the patriarch and the founder of the Hebrew race, while for the Muslims the very religion of Islam is the religion of Abraham[(s)].[37] The Prophet Abraham[(s)] is thus a strong sentimental as well as theological link between Judaism and Islam – a link which has expressed itself in the form of many common beliefs and practices. The tradition of animal sacrifice and the method of slaughter are the two spheres of influence which are generally supposed to be analogous between the two religions, but in fact they are not.

There is no suggestion in the Qur'ān or in any other of the Islamic sources that eating of meat is good for physical or spiritual health. Islam's approach in this matter is neutral; it has left the choice to the individual to be a vegetarian or a meatarian. There are many devout Muslims in the world who do not eat meat and no one ever doubts their faith. Even those who opt to eat meat are urged in the Qur'ān to eat in moderation.[38] Furthermore, there are elaborate and stringent laws governing the overall treatment of animals – their rearing and breeding; the pre-slaughter, during and after-slaughter handling – which are very different from the Judaic laws. It is a sad thing to see that the education of Muslim masses in Islamic countries in such laws leaves much to be desired. One cannot blame non-Muslims for not knowing the details of the Islamic teachings in this respect; in fact even some Muslims themselves do not know enough about them. This lack of knowledge has resulted in some serious misunderstandings about Islam in the West as well as misconceptions among Muslims themselves.

Islam has given all sentient creatures a status much higher than is generally conceded to them. There are so many verses of the Qur'ān and so many *Aḥādīth* on this theme that it would take a voluminous work to cover all of them. Some aspects of this subject have already been discussed in Chapter One. Some stipulations laid down by Islam to the method of slaughter and the pre-slaughter treatment are the essential pre-requisites of permission to eat meat. Religious discipline, like any other discipline, defeats its purpose if those who profess to accept it fail to grasp the essence of its spirit which is meant to influence the mental and moral aptitude. Such people need better education in their religion. Then, there are those who are mentally capable of grasping the spirit of the discipline and do profess to accept its principles, but start picking and choosing parts of it to suit their personal convenience. However, the most censurable are the ones who, knowingly and wilfully, ignore or stretch the law for monetary gain. Even in some Islamic countries these days conditions pertaining to the pre-slaughter handling of animals and the act of slaughter are far from satisfactory. In some cases they are even in open violation of the dictates of Islam. Of course the stipulation of invoking the name of God (*Tasmiyah* and *Takbīr*) is being meticulously carried out in Islamic abattoirs, but not enough attention is paid to the rest of the details. Even some of the professional slaughtermen are not given adequate instruction in the code of the Islamic laws in this respect.[39] Comparatively, conditions in Jewish abattoirs are much better organised than in Islamic ones.

The important point to note is that Islam has left the option of eating meat to one's discretion, subject to the limits of one's realistic needs and genuine circumstances. Had Islam laid down a categorical imperative prohibiting meat consumption, it would have gone beyond the bounds of practicability for some. However, this consideration of Islam for human physical needs goes only as far as the consumption of meat is concerned; it does not apply to the rules governing the treatment of animals during their rearing and general handling, nor does it apply to the strict laws and regulations governing the humane method of slaughter. All such injunctions are obligatory and must be carried out in every detail before the flesh of the animal becomes lawful and pure (*Ḥalāl* and *Ṭayyib*) for consumption. The Islamic permission to eat meat does not mean that one must eat it. It simply means that it may be eaten. There are many things which have not been forbidden by Islam as food, yet we have stopped eating them because modern scientific know-how has discovered better alternatives.

The real problem is that general members of the Muslim public who buy their meat from the shops in their countries never get a chance to see for themselves the un-Islamic and inhumane scenes within some of their slaughter-houses. If they knew what was happening there, they would either stop eating meat or, at least, start lobbying the powers that be to have the Islamic rules implemented.

The Qur'ān allows Muslims to eat meat slaughtered by Jews, as mentioned earlier. Both religions invoke God's name before slaughter; both have been prescribed a method of slaughter with a view to allowing the blood to drain out; and both have been charged with the moral responsibility of not taking the life of an animal except for the legitimate and imperious necessities of life. It all sounds very well in theory, but how it is being worked out in practice is a different matter.

According to the Hebrew Bible, all mankind and all species of animals were vegetarians to begin with.[40] The first recorded permission to the Israelites to eat meat was given through the Prophet Noah (Nūḥ)[(s)] after the Flood when God told him:

> "Each living animal is given to you [to eat] like the grass is given to you".[41]

Some Jewish scholars suggest that permission to eat meat was granted to the Israelites as a concession and a compromise to their weakness and that, after the advent of the Promised Messiah, the Jews would be made to become vegetarians again.[42] During their Exodus from Egypt under the conduct of Moses[(s)] the Israelites were forbidden to eat meat, except those portions of the sacrificed animals which were not offered to God at the altar. After travelling for fourteen years, they entered Israel or Yisrael in Hebrew – a name given to this region after Jacob (Ya'qūb)[(s)], according to the Biblical story, wrestled with an angel.[43] After Jacob's[(s)] encounter with the Angel, they were given permission again to use animals for food, including domestic animals. This time, however, the permission was qualified with the condition that the animal must be slaughtered 'ritually'.[44]

What Muslims understand from this condition of 'ritual slaughter' is that the Israelites were told to keep in mind, while cutting the throat of a creature of God, that permission to do so had been granted as a special Covenant in which God has laid down certain conditions to be fulfilled by man. The invocation of God's name before slaughter is to remind oneself of those conditions. The same thing applies to the invocation of Allah's name as *Takbīr*. The main reason for this condition was that, in those days, it was a common practice among the idolatrous pagans to kill animals in various cruel ways and to leave the carcasses at the altars for the deities. The monotheistic concept of God becomes meaningless if the name of a deity or any other name were to be invoked instead, especially at the most pensive moment of taking the life of a creature of God. Except for this moral consideration, there is no ceremonial or rubrical service involved in the act of slaughter. Through the passage of time, however, the Rabbinical adjuncts to the law have changed this simple act into a complex mysterious sacrament whose sacredness is liable to be broken by the slightest modification to the traditional method of slaughter. Unfortunately, some Muslims too are making this clerical error in their approach to this problem.

From the Islamic point of view there is no ritual to be observed in the slaughter of an animal. It is just a simple and straightforward, albeit a very serious, act performed to satisfy the physical need for food. The method of slaughter prescribed by both these religions was in those days, and still is, the most efficacious way to draw out blood from the body of the victim. The question whether or not pre-slaughter stunning interferes with the methods of religious slaughter is undoubtedly an important subject for discussion. Blood has been forbidden to both Jews and Muslims simply because it is unhygienic as food. We are concerned that some Muslims are falling into the same habit of adherence to the letter of the law, at the cost of its spirit.

One could give numerous examples of how some Muslims have bandied dialectic niceties in their law (*Fiqh*) to make minute distinctions without a difference. However, the matter in hand is to see how far the ardent followers of these two great religions are conforming to the humane laws of slaughter; and more consequently, how far they are conforming to the spirit of these laws instead of the letter.

Muslims should consider themselves lucky that the Qur'ān was written down by scribes during the lifetime of the Holy Prophet Muḥammad(s) *in toto* and that there is no possibility of a variant reading in its text. Throughout the 23 years' period of its revelation in Makka and Madina, the Holy Prophet(s) used to follow the practice of dictating every fresh recitation to the scribes, who used to remain in attendance in the adjoining mosque, with instructions where to collate the new verse. These scribes were called *Aṣḥāb al-ṣuffah*.[45] In addition to writing it down, people started to memorise the Qur'ān not only to recite it among other local Muslims, but also to convey it to people abroad during their travels. They were called *Qurrā'* (plural of Qāri'), or *Ḥuffāẓ* (plural of *Ḥāfiẓ*). As a further precaution to preserve the purity of the text, it was enjoined that portions of the Qur'ān be recited by the Imāms during the daily prayers. Thus even today, we hear the recitation in millions of mosques throughout the world.[46]

While all these measures have succeeded in making sure that the original words of the text remain immutable and invariable, some of our theologians have succeeded in confusing the sense of even simple verses by their micrographic glossaries. The simple, straightforward and practicable dietary laws too have not escaped the flourishes of their pens. There is a prophecy of the Holy Prophet Muḥammad(s) to the effect that a time would come when the followers of his faith would no longer remain in touch with the spirit of the Qur'ān.[47] It is high time for the general Muslims to give this prophecy serious thought and for Muslim theologians to do some introspection.

The issue of vegetarianism and meatarianism in the Jewish scriptures is so involved that one becomes confused whether or not one should eat meat at all. We have given earlier the views of some Jewish authorities that Israelites were given permission to eat meat as a concession to their weakness. This view begs the assumption that the weakness for which this concession was made is still persisting among Jews. If not, then the concessive clause becomes nullified and they should stop eating meat. We have also mentioned earlier the view of some Jewish theologians that one of the reforms which shall be made by the Promised Messiah would be to abolish the malpractice of meat eating. If the Jews do believe that it is a malpractice, why not start purifying themselves now for the Advent of the Messiah by stopping meat-eating? Some Jewish theologians have put the point in much stronger terms. They assert:

> "If the Torah (the books of Moses(s) in the Hebrew Bible) allows the use of meat, it is only for people whose spirit is lost anyway."[48]

> "Killing of animals in order to consume their meat causes damage to the human spirit."[49]

At the same time, there are other paradoxically conflicting views:

> "Meat should be consumed especially by people who are engaged in spiritual work.[50] Or: "... [meat] should be used at times when people work with their spirit such as Sabbath [Saturday] and holy days."[51]

> "The use of meat is a positive thing. ... it brings the protein of the animal from the lower level of animal protein to a higher level of human protein."[52]

There are people in this world who kill animals by subjecting them to protracted torture to make palatable relishes and patties. There are those who exploit them commercially; or others who put them on the rack in the name of pecuniary science and other ostensible stakes. From the religious point of view, all such people are committing sins; but more sinful than all of them are those who commit an act of cruelty to animals in the name of God and start quoting His scriptures to justify their iniquities.

Muslims are supposed to have a greater responsibility towards animals and are more accountable for their wrongs to them – because the Qur'ān and the teachings of the Holy Prophet Muḥammad[(s)] have left them with far more detailed instructions on animal rights and on man's moral obligations towards them than any other scripture. Islam has tried to free its adherents from all sorts of rites, rituals and ostentatious ceremonies associated with animals or their slaughter for food. Islam's extraordinary emphasis on animal welfare should have made the Muslims more capable of critical judgement and discernment in their treatment of animals – free from heresy and affected puritanism.

REFERENCES AND NOTES

1. Marcus Tullius Cicero, Roman orator, statesman and a man of letters; (143-106 B.C.).
2. These and other such examples have been cited by Jon Wynne-Tyson in: *Food for a Future*; Centaur Press, England, 1979. (Hereafter referred to as Tyson).
3. Tyson; (see Ref. No. 2, chapt. 2.); pp. 16-19, 22, 23, 36, 145.
4. In addition to Tyson's book mentioned in Ref. No. 2, the interested reader would find the following books informative on the subject: (1) *The Civilised Alternative* (see Ref. No. 2). (2) *The Composition of Foods*; R. A. McCance and E. M. Widdowson; HMSO; 1973. (3) *Food Fit for Humans*; Frank Wilson; Daniel; 1975. (4) *Eating for*

Life; Nathaniel Altman, Theosophical Publishing House; 1973. (5) *Abstinence from Animal Food*; Porphyry; Centaur Press, England; 1965. Editor's Note: A useful recent summary of statistical information on this subject can be found in 'The Global Benefits of Eating Less Meat' published CIWF Trust, River Court, Mill Lane, Godalming, Surrey GU7 1EZ, UK. See the websites: *URL:<http://www.ciwf.org.uk>* or *URL: <http://www.eatlessmeat.org>*

5. cf. *The Analects of Confucius*; Arthur Waley; New York; 1938; p.128.
6. ibid; p.150.
7. Mencius (372-285 B.C.) is considered to be the greatest exponent of the teachings of Confucius: the Neo-Confucian Movement which was started in the 13th century B.C. drew its inspiration from his teachings.
8. *Meng-tzu, The Four Books*; James Legge; Chinese Book Co., Shanghai; 1930; p.453.
9. cf. *Encyclopaedia of Buddhism*, "*Animals*"; Government Press, Ceylon; 1965.
10. *Rock Edict I*; Amulayachandra Sen; The Institute of Indology; 1956; p.64.
11. id. Malalasekara; (see Ref. No. 9).
12. *Jataka Tales*; H. Francis & E. T. Thomas; Cambridge University Press; 1916; pp. 20-22.
13. *Studies in Jaina Philosophy*; *Acaranga Sutra*; Wathmal Tatia; Jain Cultural Research Society, Banaras; 1951 p.18.
14. *Ancient Buddhism in Japan*; N. V. De Visser; Leiden; E. J. Brill; 1935; p.198.
15. cf. *The Conception of Ahimsa in Indian Thought*; Koshlya Wadia; Varanasi, Bharata Manisha; 1974.
16. cf. *Purusartha-Siddhyupaya,* p.140.
17. *P. S. Jaini*; p.171.
18. cf. *Jaina Sutra*; Herman Jacobi; Motilal Banarsidas, Delhi; 1973.
19. *The Buddha Speaks the Brahma Net Sutra*; Buddhist Text Translation Society, Talmage, California; p.150.
20. *Vinaya Texts*; T. W. Rhys-Davids & Herman Oldenberg; Motilal Banarsidas, Delhi; 1974.
21. ibid. (see Ref. No. 9).
22. *Universal Responsibility and the Good Heart*; Tanzin Gyatso, the 14th Dalai Lama, Library of Tibetan Works, India; 1980; p.78.
23. *Genesis*; 1:29, 30.
24. *Leviticus*; 2:1.
25. *Christ in Christian Tradition*; Aloys Grillemier; Mowbrays; 1965.
26. *Church Dogmatics*; Karl Barth; Vol. III, Part One, T. & T. Clark; 1958; p.208.

27. *Isaiah*; 22:13, 14.
28. *Isaiah*; 65:17-25.
29. *Isaiah*; 11:6.
30. For detailed views of Jewish vegetarianism, refer to *The Prophecy of Vegetarianism and Peace* by Rabbi Hochen-Knock – the first Chief Rabbi of Israel. Also contact the Jewish Vegetarian Society, "Bet Jeva", 855 Finchley Road, London NW11. There have been three vegetarian Chief Rabbis in Israel during the last 25 years. (The quotations have been taken from their literature.)
31. The Qur'ān; 3:64; Free translation by: Mawlānā Abū'l-Kalām Āzād; *Tarjumān al-Qur'ān,* Vol. 2; Asia Publishing House; London; 1967.
32. Ḥadīth: *Ṣaḥīḥ al-Bukhārī*: 1:1 Imām 'Abdullāh Muḥammad ibn Ismā'īl al-Bukhārī; Krehl & Juynboll, Leiden; 1908.
33. The Qur'ān; 5:6 (some translations, 5:5).
34. *Deuteronomy*; 7:2, 3.
35. The Qur'ān; 2:190; 8:61, 62; 22:39.
36. The Qur'ān; 22:40. (For the details of the Caliph Abū Bakr's instructions to the army cf. *Ṭabarī*, III, p.123.)
37. The Qur'ān; 3:66.
38. The Qur'ān; 7:31; 5:87; and other verses.
39. The writer is basing this statement on his personal visits to about 45 countries, most of which were Islamic.
40. *Genesis*; 1:29, 30 & *Isaiah*; 11:6-9.
41. *Genesis*; 1:29, 30.
42. Rabbi Abraham Kood, the Chief Rabbi of Palestine before the establishment of the state of Israel.
43. *Genesis*; 32:28.
44. *Genesis*; 32:32.
45. (1) *Ḥadīth*: *Kitāb al-Sunan*, 2:123; Abū Dāwūd Sulaymān.
    (2) *Ḥadīth*: *al-Jāmi' al-Musnad al-Ṣaḥīḥ,* Bukhārī, 66:4.
    (3) ibid. 65:19, 20.
    (4) Imām Ibn Ḥajar al-'Asqalānī has mentioned many scribes by name, including the first four Caliphs: Abū Bakr (632 A.C. – 11 A.H.); 'Umar ibn al-Khaṭṭāb (634 A.C. – 13 A.H.); 'Uthmān (644 A.C. – 23 A.H.); 'Alī ibn Abī Ṭālib (656 A.C. – 35 A.H.) in his book of *Ḥadīth*: *Fatḥ al-Bārī fī Sharḥ Ṣaḥīḥ al-Bukhārī.*

46. *Ḥadīth*: *Ṣaḥīḥ al-Bukhārī*, 3:27; 66:21-23, 25, 33. (see Ref. No. 32).
47. *Ḥadīth*: *Al-Jāmi'*, 39:5; Abū 'Īsā al-Tirmidhī.
48. cf. *Abarbanel* 1610; as quoted in *Jewish Attitude Towards Slaughter*; I. M. Levinger; Department of Life Sciences, Bar Ilan University, Ramat Gan, Israel; Animal Regulation Studies, 2, (1979) 103-109, Elsevier Scientific Publishing Co., Amsterdam.
49. *Albo*, 1425. (see Ref. No. 48).
50. *Talmud*, (see Ref. No. 48).
51. *Maimonides*, 1150 b; (see Ref. No. 48).
52. *Machmanides*, 1250; (see Ref. No. 48).

CHAPTER THREE

ANIMAL SACRIFICE

Preamble

THE CONCEPT OF animal sacrifice goes as far back as recorded history. During the early stages of man's awareness of a psychic force within himself the primordial concept of sacrifice was that of thanking the supernatural forces and to appease their anger by atonement, while the archaic concept of the supernatural was that of astral beings which could take physical forms and, like human beings, had corporeal needs which had to be satisfied. In order to express obeisance to these beings, man started making tangible and visible symbols to represent these imaginary beings in the form of idols. The deities and spirits had to be kept happy by offerings of gifts, such as food and drink, or other prized possessions of man.

The concept of sacrifice in the name of gods and deities has passed through various stages and forms of development. The fear of the unknown and the unsubduable elements of nature created feelings of frustration and helplessness which, in turn, demanded submissiveness and self-denial. Primitive man could think of no other way of keeping the astral spirits happy except by offering them the things he prized in his own life. The sentiment of sacrifice, however, remains unfulfilled unless it is enacted ostentatiously in the form of ritual and ceremony. The history of religion shows that, during the early stages, ritual was considered to be the most important part of worship – mostly through sacrifice.

Most commentators of the Scriptures, especially modern theologians, have tried to explain away their respective sacrificial traditions in terms of symbolic worship of God. Some religions have declared animal sacrifice as a means of atonement by transferring one's sins to an animal as if God was incapable of forgiving man's sins without punishing someone, even though it were an innocent substitute for the sinner. In this day and age there are still people who believe that blood is the sacred token of life. Primitive man used to shed human blood as an offering to his gods, deities and numerous other astral spirits. Modern man claims that he has become more civilised and rational. He offers to his God animal flesh and blood instead.

THE ANCIENT ORIENT

For the last six thousand years the Vedic doctrine of *Ahimsā* has played a very significant role not only in the matter of sacrifice, but also in the general attitude towards animals. *Ahimsā* is generally translated as 'non-injury' but it means much more than that. It covers the negation of animosity (*Avera*) and ill-will (*Abyapajja*) as well as positive feelings of fraternity (*Mettacitta*). However, this doctrine has not succeeded in abolishing animal sacrifice to the same extent as it has promoted vegetarianism, which has already been discussed in Chapter Two.

CONFUCIANISM

According to Taylor, sacrificial feasts used to be officially celebrated in China during the time of Confucius.[1] Confucius rejected the suggestion of a disciple, Tzu-Kung, that the practice of offering a sheep as a sacrifice at every new moon be discontinued. His verdict was that ritual (*Li*) was more important than sheep and said to Tzu-Kung:

> "you grudge sheep, but I grudge ritual".[2]

Again he has been recorded in the Analects as saying:

> "I believe in and have a passion for [the ways of] the ancients".[3]

HINDUISM

Numerically Hindus form the majority of the followers of Vedic Scriptures, although it is suggested by some that Hinduism is only a derivative branch of the original Vedic religion. Every act in the life of a Hindu, whether religious or secular, is governed by some sort of prophetic signification of omens and portents through ritual, some of which even involve animal sacrifice. The Mogul Emperor Akbar attempted to stop the practice of human sacrifice when Hindu widows were burned alive on the funeral pyres of their husbands as *suttees* or *satees*. Later the British Raj had to pass strict laws to abolish the custom. Since independence, the Government of India has been trying to ban the practice of animal sacrifice, yet the traditional custom still continues in certain places.

The writer once happened to witness a bull-sacrifice some sixty years ago in an Indian State called Chumba, in the Himachal Pradesh range of mountains about 25 miles north of Dalhousie. It was an ultra orthodox Hindu State, so much so that even to boo a cow or bull in the street was considered sacrilegious. Paradoxically, however, the same cow-worshippers used to throw a bull once a year down the cliffs into the tributary of a river as a sacrifice to the goddess of water. On this occasion the garlanded bull was led to the cliff-edge by a choir of laudative pundits, followed by a fanfare of trumpets and horns. After a long session of intonations and incantations, the legs of the bull were strapped and the poor animal was shoved over the cliff. The bull started tumbling down, the cascade of water knocking it about from boulder to boulder, until a bend in the gorge hid it from view. Everyone present raised his hands and eyes upwards as if to say to the goddess above the clouds:

> "See, how good we are! We have done our duty. Now it is up to you to look after us until this day next year – *Om, Shanti, Hari Om* – Great is the Trinity of Vishnu, Siva and Brahma, Peace; Long live the Trinity."

JAINISM

As mentioned earlier, Jainism is supposed to be an offshoot of Hinduism but with much more stringent dietetic laws than those of the general body of Hinduism. Being staunch vegetarians and believers in *Ahimsā* to the letter, they totally reject the very concept of animal sacrifice. Their verdict can best be summed up in these words from the Yogasastra:

> "Those inconsiderate people who sacrifice animals as an offering to gods are devoid of tender feelings and mercy and are doomed to destruction."[4]

BUDDHISM

The Buddhists too do not believe in animal sacrifice as such. Some of them do eat meat, but it does not involve any ritualistic killing nor do they make animals into scapegoats for atonement. Their concept of sacrifice is based on reciprocity by way of voluntary interchange of life between man and beast, as discussed previously. Some examples of this kind of mutual sacrifice are found in their scriptures.[5] In spite of many differences, Buddhism has one very significant principle in common with Islam, that is: not to lay down any categorical laws which cannot be observed; and to follow the "Middle Path", known in Islam as *"al-ṭarīq al-wusṭā"*.

CHRISTIANITY

The Christian concept that Christ[(s)] allowed himself to be sacrificed at the Cross, as the "lamb of God", to redeem the world of its sins leaves no scope for any scapegoat to take over the Christians' sins nor the sacrifice of any animal for atonement.

The doctrine of 'Cosmic Christ', although based on a very different theology from that of the Buddhist and the general Hindu *Vedanta*, has led to the Christian belief in the presence of God even in animals. Certain passages in the

Old Testament do give the impression that all animals have been created merely for the benefit of human species and that man has the divine-given right to sacrifice them at the altar of his needs. However, Christians have started interpreting such passages in the context of Cosmic Christology. The practical examples set by the Christian saints have been greatly responsible for the creation of a sense of affinity between man and other sentient beings.

The very image of the baby-Christ lying in the manger of a stable cements that sense of affinity. St. Hubert, the hunter, saw the image of Christ[s] in a stag and refrained from shooting it. The 'little poor man', St. Francis of Assisi (12th Century), used to talk to animals and preach sermons to the birds – although it is said that he used to eat meat. Many of the Christian saints were such fervent animal lovers that they have gone down in history as their patrons. St. Benedict has been associated with ravens; St. Ulrich with rats; St. Bridget with ducks; St. Menas with camels; and so on. The British Government passed the first law against cruelty to animals in 1822. It is not generally known, however, that six hundred years earlier St. Francis had entreated the Roman Emperor to pass a similar law. About four centuries ago St. Martin de Porres, opened a hospital for animals. He was a Spanish prince by a negro mother. St. Paul, while talking of suffering in the world, talks of all creation and not of mankind alone in these words:

> "for we know that the whole creation groaneth and travaileth in pain together until now. And not only they, but ourselves also, which have the first fruits of the Spirit, even we ourselves groan with ourselves ...".[6]

JUDAISM

Muslims in general know very little about Judaism as a religion. Their general impression is that Islam is a continuation of the Prophet Abraham's[s] creed; that both Islam and Judaism are the true monotheistic religions; that marriages with Jewish women are allowed; and, most relevantly, that Jewish food is lawful for Muslims.

It is intended in this chapter to try to put right some of their mistaken notions about Judaic theology in matters related to animal sacrifices.

THE BIBLICAL CONCEPT OF GOD

Islam came at a period of history when Judaism was well established in the Arabian Peninsula. One of the reasons why Judaism was better organised than Christianity was that all the tribes of Israel had one common ethnic origin and, hence, one common traditional source of Aramaean culture. Christianity and Islam, as opposed to that, were non-ethnic religions with their doors open to the whole world irrespective of race or colour. The Hebrews are originally Semites who were spread out as Babylonians, Assyrians, Aramaeans, Phoenicians, Edomites, Ammonites, Hebrews and Abyssinians. It is only for the last 3,000 years that the history of the Jewish people can be identified. Before the Davidic (*Dāwūd*)[(s)] period (from about 1,000 B.C.) the religion of this tribe of Hebrews which is now known as Israelites was greatly influenced by the cults of other Semitic tribes. This influence shows itself very markedly during the Hammurabi period (cir. 2,000 B.C.).

The most conspicuous feature of the concept of God in the Hebrew Bible is His physical existence, as if He were a corporeal being whose bodily needs have to be satisfied – the same as the needs of animals and human beings. He needs food and drink and enjoys the savoury smell of roasting meat. Many passages ask believers to offer to Him drink (libation) and food or bread; and depict Him as a sabre-rattling parochial God of Zion who commands His people to "subdue nations":

> "Thus said the Lord to his anointed, to Cyrus [*Kūrush*], whose right hand I have holden, to subdue nations before him."[7]

> "Proclaim ye this among the gentiles; Prepare war, ... The Lord also shall roar out of Zion... So shall ye know that I am the Lord your God

> dwelling in Zion, my holy Mountain: then shall Jerusalem be holy and no strangers pass through her any more."[8]

Originally simple water used to be offered to God at the altar, but later wine was substituted.[9] In some versions of the Bible even the word 'strong wine' has been used. It is interesting to note that the wine was not wasted by splashing it against the altar like the blood of sacrificial animals. The wine-jars were waved symbolically at the altar and the wine saved to be drunk by the priests.

It was only at a later stage that the Deuteronomic law sanctioned the consumption of meat, otherwise, before that all slaughter was a sacrifice as God's food.[10] The Bible calls the portions of meat burnt on the altar as the 'Lord's food or bread';[11] the altar as the 'Lord's table'.[12] Even the utensils used for the rites in the tabernacle are called the 'Lord's vessels and pots'. According to Leviticus, only the male children of Aaron could eat portions of some offerings and the rest was God's share.[13] Whenever a burnt offering is mentioned, it is clear that the Lord enjoys the 'sweet savoury smell' of burning meat. Out of numerous such quotations, one about Noah[(s)] (*Nūḥ*) would be of more interest to Muslims:

> "And Noah builded an altar unto the Lord; and took of every clean beast, and of every clean fowl and offered burnt offerings on the altar. And the Lord smelled a sweet savour; ... ."[14]

Another interesting definition of God is that of the Cabalist Jews. According to them *Sekinah* represents the masculine and the feminine natures of the divine world. Talmud, Midrash and the Targums[15] speak of *Sekinah* as an intermediary between God and the world of nature, including mankind, through which God rules the world. It also works as the uniting force between God and the priest who performs the sacrifice. *Sekinah*'s feminine gender is represented by *Sefirah Malkhut* while *Sefirah Tiferet* is her husband. The union between husband and wife, or between the masculine and feminine in the divine world is brought about through the blood of sacrificed animals. More importantly, slaughter is a sort of favour to the animal because it releases its spirit and enables it to return to its origin.

The Cabalists believe that sacrifices help 'good' to overpower 'evil' in the universal struggle between the two. This is carried still further in their belief that sacrifices are shared between Satan (*Sitra Ohra*) and God. The flesh serves as food for the evil powers of cosmos, while God receives the good intentions of the person who offers the sacrifice. The scapegoat sacrifice on the Day of Atonement, however, is meant exclusively to placate the evil powers.[16]

Before Israel, the Babylonians and Mesopotamians used to call their chief deity *Yahwe*. The word 'Yah' stands for the supreme astral being. Later the Israelites adopted this name for their God and by reading the Hebrew Bible it would seem that some of the attributes assigned to the pre-Israelite *Yahwe* have influenced their concept of God.

CONCEPTS OF GOD

Monotheism and polytheism are separated by a hair's breadth. An earnest study of the Hebrew Bible leaves no doubt that its revealed text has been so mixed up with the Rabbinical appendages that the two have become inseparable. In Judaism, at every step and on every occasion Divine worship had to be augmented with offerings – especially burnt offerings of animals. This kind of symbolism and ritualism appealled to the Israelites not because it was convincing to them theologically, but because their minds could not discard the pre-Judaic image of the bloodthirsty *Yahwe* – just as some Muslims have not yet been able to shake off the influences of their respective pre-Islamic cultures, even after fourteen centuries.

ATONEMENT

The Old Testament goes to great lengths to explain that atonement can be achieved through animal sacrifice and that the blood of sacrificed animals has the potency to cleanse sins. Another suggested way of getting rid of sins is by the use of a scapegoat. For example:

> "And when he hath made an end of reconciling the holy place, and the tabernacle of the congregation, and the altar [with blood], he shall bring the live goat: and Aaron shall lay both his hands upon the head of the live goat, and confess over him all the iniquities of the children of Israel and all their transgressions in all their sins, putting them [the sins] upon the head of the goat, and shall send him [the goat] away by the hand of a fit man into the wilderness: and the goat shall bear upon him all their iniquities unto a land not inhabited: and he shall let go the goat in the wilderness."[17]

> "And Aaron shall cast lots upon the two goats; one lot for the Lord, and the other lot for the scapegoat."[18]

These and many other such passages give the impression that sins are like a bundle of nettles which can be transferred from one's back onto that of a goat. The very word 'scapegoat' owes its origin to this practice.

THE JUDAIC THEOLOGY OF SACRIFICE

The Jewish belief in the importance of animal sacrifice goes as far back as the two sons of Adam. Both Cain and Abel (Qābīl and Hābīl) brought their offerings to the Lord; Cain offered fruit and Abel offered animals. The result is very significant:

> "And the Lord had respect unto Abel and to his offering; but unto Cain and to his offering he had no respect."[19]

Since then all the Biblical prophets have been recorded as offering animal sacrifices at the altars:

> "And Noah builded an altar unto the Lord; and took of every clean beast, and of every clean fowl and offered burnt offerings on the altar. And the Lord smelled a sweet savour; and the Lord said in his heart, I will not again curse the ground any more for man's sake."[20]

Job (Ayyūb) of Uz was a "perfect and upright" man who "feared God and eschewed evil". He had seven sons and three daughters. In order to sanctify them he continually offered 'burnt offerings' of one animal for each child.[21] God's "wrath was kindled" against three people named Eliphaz, Bildad and Zophar. By way of punishment the Lord commanded these three people: "take unto you now seven bullocks and seven rams, and go to my servant Job, and offer up for yourselves a burnt offering; and my servant Job shall pray for you."[22] Jacob (Ya'qūb) is also recorded as having made a sacrifice called *Zevahim* to seal a promise which he had given to Laban that he would not "afflict" his daughter in his absence.[23] Another occasion when he offered *Zevahim* sacrifices was at Beer-Sheba.[24] Whenever the Prophet Abraham[(s)] migrated to a new place, he did two things: "he called upon the name of God" and "there he builded an altar unto the Lord".[25] He is recorded as having made not ordinary but burnt offerings on those altars.[26] Many other patriarchs are also recorded as following the same practice. Issac (Isḥāq) glorified the name of the Lord and built altars for burnt sacrifices.[27]

Building altars and offering animal sacrifices was an integral part of the prophets' worship, wherever they went.[28]

THE CULTUS OF SACRIFICE

All the Biblical books, starting from the patriarchal scriptures, lay great emphasis on ritual and ceremony. The very word used for Judaic worship is derived from the Latin word *'cultus'* which generally means the worship of a deity in the form of external ritual and ceremony, as distinguished from the intrinsic spirit of worship.

This subject deserves more than mere academic interest because of the enormity of carnage this mode of worship resulted in. Animals not in thousands but in millions; not for food but to appease – were slaughtered and turned to cinders.

The Jewish festivals are divided into many categories. Some are Propitiary for the appeasement of the offended God, such as the guilt and sin offerings (*'Asham* and *Hall'at*). Some are Dedicatory, mostly in the form of communal sacrifices.[29] Then there are burnt-sacrifices (*ha-tamid* and *olah*) to God. They have to be continual – one in the morning and one in the evening, with additional weekly sacrifices on Sabbaths, and monthly sacrifices on New Moon and other moon-festivals and holy days.[30]

BIBLICAL CONDEMNATION OF SACRIFICE

There are many antitheses in the Hebrew Bible about sacrifice. There are numerous passages accentuating the importance of sacrifice as a means of atonement while, at the same time, the following passages speak in terms of condemnation of it:

> "To what purpose is the multitude of your sacrifices unto me? saith the Lord: I am full of the burnt offerings of rams, and the fat of the fed beasts; and I delight not in the blood of bullocks, or of lambs, or of the goats.... Bring me no more vain oblations; ...: I am weary to bear them. ... Your hands are full of blood ... ."[31]

> "O Ephraim, what shall I do unto thee? O Juda, what shall I do unto thee? for your goodness is as a morning cloud, and as the early dew it goeth away ... For I desired mercy, and not sacrifice; and the knowledge of God more than burnt offerings."[32]

> "Woe unto you that desire the day of the Lord! to what end is it for you? the day of the Lord is darkness, and not light. ... . I hate, I despise

your feast days, and I will not smell in your solemn assemblies. Though ye offer me burnt offerings and your meat offerings I will not accept them: neither will I regard the peace offerings of your fat beasts."[33]

In the following verse, a very clear-cut message is conveyed, laying down the basic principles about animal sacrifice that God does not disapprove of sacrifices provided the meat is put to some good use; that He disapproves of the wastage of meat which is mistakenly believed to be God's share; that God does not feel hungry and does not eat flesh, nor does he drink blood; and finally, that the only sensible way to offer thanks to God for His bounties is by living up to the vows you have taken unto Him through the Covenant:

"O Israel, and I will testify against thee: I am God, even thy God. I will not reprove thee for thy sacrifices or thy burnt offerings, to have been continually before me. I will take no bullock out of thy house, nor the goats out of thy folds. For every beast of the forest is mine. And the cattle upon a thousand hills. I know all the fowls of the mountains. And the wild beasts of the field are mine. If I were hungry, I would not tell thee. For the world is mine, and the fullness thereof. Will I eat flesh of bulls. Or drink the blood of goats? Offer unto God thanksgiving. And pay thy vows unto the most High."[34]

This message of the Hebrew Bible was repeated centuries later in the Qur'ān in these words:

"*It is not their flesh, nor their blood, that reaches Allah; it is your righteousness [piety and spiritual volition] that reaches Him ....*" (Qur'ān 22:37).

The Islamic concept of sacrifice will be discussed in some detail later in this chapter. Meanwhile, the following Biblical quotation emphasises the same message:

"Thus saith the Lord of hosts, the God of Israel; Put your burnt offerings unto your sacrifices, and eat flesh ... ."[35]

Maimonides[36] and other classicists have expressed the view that the Israelites at the time of Moses[(s)] were not ready to give up sacrificial practices, therefore God allowed them to continue with them. In spite of all this disapprobation and reproof, the Israelites continued the sacrificial tradition – each new generation of priests adding to the involved intricacies for ritual.

After the fall of Jerusalem and the destruction of the Temple in 66 A.C. it was no longer possible to continue with the daily *Tamid* and other sacrifices. Instead, special prayer services, called *Shaharit, Minha* and *Musaf,* were introduced.[37] However the Jewish tradition of animal sacrifice was so strong that a special prayer was added to the Amidah prayer for the re-introduction of sacrifice. Joseph Hertz, while explaining the reason, says:

"Moderns do not always realize the genuine hold the sacrificial service had upon the affections of the people in ancient Israel."[38] Orthodox Jews still go on saying this additional prayer. Michael Friedlander advocated the views of the orthodoxy in 1913: "The revival of sacrificial service must, likewise, be sanctioned by the voice of a prophet ... ."[39]

Liberal Jews believe that:

"the decline which Jewish life has suffered in the last 200 years has been due in large measure to the refusal of its 'orthodox' leaders to come to terms with the modern world."[40]

Perhaps this kind of censure on Jewish orthodox leaders would inspire Muslims to take stock of their own 'orthodox' leadership. It is mostly due to its schismatic tendencies and lack of spiritual volition (*Taqwā*) that irresponsible Movements have sprung up in Islam.

THE RABBINSHIP (PRIESTHOOD)

One of the main reasons why Jews clung onto the mode of worship through sacrifice was the influence of priesthood on their religion. When salvation and atonement became attainable more through law than worship, the worship itself became difficult to follow without the guidance of priests. The shift of emphasis from the spiritual worship of God to the ever-increasing list of ceremonial rituals in the temple was responsible to a large extent in making the Jews seek atonement through sacrificial offerings – animal sacrifice claiming the highest place. A mistake in the observance of a ritualistic detail would nullify the sacrifices. Who else is there to guide a simple layman through the elaborate sacrificial procedure than the priests who are the hereditary beneficiaries of the sacrifices? In a situation like this, who can blame the Jewish laity if they unwittingly fell into the trap and got themselves entangled in the web of rituals and ceremonies?

THE MEANING OF SACRIFICE

According to the occult theosophy of the Jewish Cabalists, every letter, word, number and accent of the Hebrew Bible contains a hidden meaning. The symbolic acts associated with sacrifice have special esoteric significance for the Jews in general and for the Cabalists in particular. Some of their views throw light on the enormity of the problem which the reformers within Judaism have had to face and are facing today. According to the Cabalists, sacrifices are a link between man and God and serve as the physical media of expression for spiritual worship. Jews attach great importance to the condition that the animal must be without blemish, not only for sacrificial animals but also for those for daily consumption. Their concept of 'blemish' is very different from that of Muslims. This condition has a great bearing on the controversial issue of the method of slaughter and the use of stunners.

Man's inhumanity to man in the name of religion and God is psychologically in the historical sequence of his atrocities against the rest of the animated world. The theologians have always found some passage or other in their respective Scriptures to support their conduct both against man and beast. The Holy Office of Rome dug up enough ecclesiastical excuses in the New Testament to justify the torture of so-called heretics during the Spanish Inquisition.[41] The slave traders found their justification in the Bible to the effect that the station in life of the Negroid races was to remain hewers of wood and drawers of water.[42] Even these days there is hardly any part of the world where wars are not being fought in the name of religion – each faction soiling the pages of their Scriptures with thumb-marks to prove that theirs is the 'holy' cause. All this has happened in the past, is happening, and will go on happening, unless man starts respecting life as a whole in its entirety. For centuries prophets and sages have been warning the human species that their cruelty to animals would have a psychotic effect on their own mentality and that this would, ultimately, rebound on themselves. All the evidence in the world today shows that the reaction of cruelty to animals has started taking mankind on the rebound.

With what pathos George Bernard Shaw (1856–1950) echoes these sentiments in the following poem:

WAR – LIVING GRAVES

We are the living graves of murdered beasts,
Slaughtered to satisfy our appetites.
We never pause to wonder at our feats,
If animals, like men, can possibly have rights.
We pray on Sundays that we may have light,
To guide our footsteps on the path we tread.
We're sick of War, we do not want to fight –
The thought of it now fills our hearts with dread,
And yet – we gorge ourselves upon the dead.

Like carrion crows, we live and feed on meat,
Regardless of the suffering and pain

We cause by doing so, if thus we treat
Defenceless animals for sport or gain,
How can we hope in this world to attain
The PEACE we say we are so anxious for.
We pray for it, o'er hecatombs, of slain,
To God, while outraging the moral law.
Thus cruelty begets its offspring.[43]

ISLAM

The utilitarian value of animals and the Islamic concern for them has been discussed in Chapter One. It has been explained why Islam has not prohibited meat-eating altogether, and has left it to individual choice, needs and circumstances. In this chapter an attempt has been made to explain the Islamic concept of animal sacrifice. In order to understand that, it is necessary to deal with the subject on two levels. One is the Scriptural or canonical level, i.e. the concept of sacrifice as contained in the Islamic law or *Sharīʿah*. The second level is how that scriptural concept is being understood and practised by the various strata of Muslim society in different parts of the world. Those who feel that Islam should not have allowed animal sacrifice at all should read this chapter in conjunction with Chapter Two in which the subject of vegetarianism and meatarianism has been discussed. Accepting the fact that Islam has allowed the consumption of meat, even if wrongly from their point of view, this chapter should be read to appreciate how much Islam has tried to change the primordial concept of sacrifice by channelling it into an institution of charity. At the same time, those Muslims who are not used to taking self-criticism in good spirits should appreciate the fact that Islam is a spiritual ideology and all Muslims as its followers need not necessarily be capable of comprehending that ideology intellectually.

Islam is not a new or isolated religion. It is a continuation of all the previous monotheistic theologies which, according to the Qur'ān, have been revealed throughout the ages in all parts of the world.[44] Belief in all of them is one of the terms of faith in Islam.[45] This conception is taken so affirmatively that the creed of the Prophet Abraham[(s)], for example, is believed to be the religion of Islam. Similarly, a Muslim's faith in Islam, remains incomplete unless he or she accepts Jesus Christ[(s)] also as a Messenger of God and The Messiah (*Al-Masīḥ*).[46]

THE PRELUDE TO ISLAMIC SACRIFICE

It was with this kind of religious background that Islam continued with the tradition of animal sacrifice. First, it is important to study the Qur'ānic version of the Prophet Abraham's[(s)] sacrifice, which is the basic source of the Islamic concept of sacrifice. The Prophet Abraham[(s)] was commanded by God to sacrifice his son. Both father and son agreed to carry out the command, but at the last moment, God called out to Abraham[(s)] to stop, saying:

> "*You have indeed fulfilled the vision [by showing your willingness to sacrifice your son]. Thus do We reward the righteous. This was obviously a great trial – and We ransomed him with a momentous sacrifice, and left him, thus, for posterity to say in laudation: 'Peace be upon him.'*" (Qur'ān 37:105–109).

Muslims understand from this incident that:

a. It serves as a supreme example of man's submission to the will of God.
b. During that period of history, human sacrifice was quite a common practice all over the world. All the races of ancient Greece, such as the Minoan, the Mycenaean and the Pelasgians of the Mediterranean race, used to offer human sacrifices regularly. The practice remained persistently in vogue during the much later period of their partial domination by the Achaean and the Dorian tribes throughout the mainland of Greece. Even the Hellenic period from the first Olympiad (776-5 B.C.) to the death of Alexander (320 B.C.) was not free from this abominable practice.[47] The same was the case with the Babylonians and the other Semitic tribes, including the Hebrews.[48] God's act of

ransoming Abraham's[(s)] son with a ram was meant, according to Muslims, to serve as a prohibition of human sacrifices.

c. Most Muslim commentators of the Qur'ān suggest that the word 'momentous' (*'Aẓīm*) in the verse:

"*We ransomed him with a momentous sacrifice*" (Qur'ān 37:107)

and the promise that posterity will always send blessings on Abraham[(s)] signify the commemoration of that great man's willingness to cut the throat of that son for whom he had prayed so earnestly to get. It is to celebrate this that the Festival of Sacrifice (*'Īd al-Aḍḥā*) is held annually and animals are sacrificed for distribution among the poor. The Holy Prophet Muḥammad[(s)] was once asked by his Companions why animal sacrifice was allowed to be continued in Islam. He replied:

> "This is a commemorative tradition (*Sunnah*) of your patriarch Abraham."[49]

The invocation of God's blessings on the Prophet Abraham[(s)] has since been an integral part of the prescribed mode of worship during the ten days of pilgrimage in the form of the following oft-repeated prayer:

> "O Allah! Exalt Muḥammad and the posterity of Muḥammad, as You did exalt Abraham and the posterity of Abraham: You are Praiseworthy and Glorious. O Allah! Bless Muḥammad and the posterity of Muḥammad, as You did bless Abraham and the posterity of Abraham; You are Praiseworthy and Glorious."

The importance that Muslims attach to the Prophet Abraham[(s)] and his sacrifice can be appreciated from the fact that the above prayer is also repeated many times a day by all Muslims in their congregational as well as in other individual prayers. There is another association between the animal sacrifices during the pilgrimage and the Prophet Abraham[s]. It is based on a prayer of Abraham[s] recorded in the Qur'ān. When he took abode in the valley of Makka with his wife and son, he prayed:

"*Our Lord! I have settled some of my offspring in a barren valley near Thy sacred House so that, O our Sustainer! they might keep up their prayers. Cause Thou, therefore, people's hearts to incline towards them and provide them with fruitful sustenance, that they may be grateful.*" (Qur'ān 14:37)

THE ISLAMIC THEOLOGY OF SACRIFICE

The tradition of animal sacrifice in Islam is based mainly on the following verses of the Qur'ān:

"*When We assigned unto Abraham the site of this House* [*of* Ka'bah], *We said 'Do not ascribe divinity to aught beside Me, and sanctify My House for those who walk around it, who stand upright and bow down and prostrate themselves in it to pray.*'" (Qur'ān 22:26)

"*Hence, O Muḥammad! proclaim among people the pilgrimage: they will come to thee on foot and on every kind of nimble-footed mounts from far and wide.*" (Qur'ān 22:27)

"*That they may avail themselves of many benefits of it and call to mind the name of Allah on the appointed days of pilgrimage over the sustenance He has provided for them in the form of flocks and herds. Eat, then, of them and feed the unfortunate poor.*" (Qur'ān 22:28)

"*And accomplish the pilgrimage* (Ḥajj) *and the Visit of the sacred places* ('Umrah) *for Allah: but if you are prevented from doing so, then send instead whatever offering is feasible. And do not shave your heads until the offering has reached its destination. He among you who is ill or suffers from some ailment of the scalp, [necessitating the shaving of the head before the appointed time], should expiate either by fasting or almsgiving or by any other form of worship. In times of peace and security – one who avails oneself of combining a Visit to the sacred places and the Pilgrimage – shall make an offering such as one can easily afford."* (Qur'ān 2:196)

"*... All cattle have been made lawful for you [as food], save those already mentioned to you [as forbidden] ... .*" (Qur'ān 22:30)

"*And for all people We have ordained acts of devotion that they might mention the name of Allah on what He has given them of the flocks and herds [for food] ... And give glad tidings to those who are ... humble ... .*" (Qur'ān 22:34)

"*Whose hearts are filled with awe at the mention of Allah ... and who expend in charity out of what We have bestowed upon them as sustenance.*" (Qur'ān 22:35)

" *... So pronounce over them the name of Allah ..., eat yourselves thereof and feed those poor who are resigned to their lot, as well as those who beg with humility. It is to this end that We have subjected animals to your needs that you may be grateful.*" (Qur'ān 22:36)

"*[Know that] neither their flesh nor their blood reaches Allah; it is only your righteousness that reaches Him. It is to this end that We have subjected animals to your needs that you may glorify Allah for His guidance to you: And give thou glad tidings to those who do good [to others].*" (Qur'ān 22:37)

"*Declare [O Muḥammad]: 'As for me, my Lord has guided me onto a right path through an ever-true religion – the creed of Abraham who was a man of pure faith and was not one of the polytheists.' Say: 'My prayer, my service of sacrifice, my living and my dying – surely all are for Allah, Who is the Lord of all the worlds.'"* (Qur'ān 6:161-162)

Muslims generally believe that the above verses lay down a canonical law to offer animal sacrifices during the festival of pilgrimage and that replacement of animals with any other kind of offering would be wrong. However, a close study of these and other such verses makes it abundantly clear that the Qur'ānic approach is not meant to take animal sacrifice as an end in itself; it is meant to be used as a means to serve a social need.

SACRIFICE AS CHARITY AND ALTERNATIVE OFFERINGS

One salient point that emerges from these verses is that the main purpose of allowing the Muslims to continue with animal sacrifices was to turn this age-old tradition into an institution of charity. Even the literal annotations which some Muslim theologians put on these verses to the effect that animal sacrifice is an act of worship and thanksgiving to God becomes valid only if sacrifice ends up as an act of charity. All the verses of the Qur'ān which deal with the subject wind up with the proviso that the meat be fed to the poor, the needy, those who are too modest to beg as well as the mendicants – those who beg openly.[50] In some cases the offerers of the sacrifice are allowed to consume a portion of the meat themselves, while in others the whole of the sacrificed animal is to be given in charity. Sacrifice is meant to be an act of worship and thanksgiving to solicit the approbation of God neither in the sense of atonement nor in the sense of transposing one's sins onto a scapegoat; but it is meant to be an act of benevolence (*Iḥsān*) to fulfil a social obligation. After reading the Qur'ānic version of sacrifice, there remains no doubt in one's mind that any sacrifice that is allowed to go to waste is a sinful as well as a criminal violation of the Islamic law (*Sharī'ah*). Verses 22:36 and 37 make this proviso abundantly clear.

The original purpose of offering gifts (*Hady*) at the sacred house (*Ka'bah*) was to succour the ancient Makkans who were the descendants of the Prophet

Abraham[(s)] in response to his prayer in verse 14:37. In those days the supply of provisions, such as meat, was their most essential need. The whole area was an arid desert. Under those circumstances it was a very sensible and practical proposition for Islam to ask pilgrims to offer gifts in the form of sacrificial animals. Today the Makkans are in a position to import their food without anybody's help, while there are millions of people in the rest of the Islamic world who are undernourished. Gifts are meant to express one's love and adoration, and are appreciated the more if they are to the recipient's taste and need and serve some useful purpose.

The Qur'ān does mention animal sacrifices to expiate (*dam*) certain offences committed during the *Ḥajj*, but at the same time it mentions alternative offerings and alternative acts of devotion. Verse 2:196 suggests fasting or almsgiving or whatever kind of offering is feasible. In the following verse the Qur'ān does mention the reason but leaves the choice of alternatives to the individual. The precincts of Makka are declared as an animal and bird sanctuary during the period of pilgrimage in the following verse:

> "*O believers! slay no game while you are in a pilgrim-sanctity. Whosoever of you slays it intentionally, shall pay the penalty by offering to the* Ka'bah *a domestic animal the like of that which he has slain – as determined by two persons of equity among you; or he shall expiate by feeding the indigent; or by keeping equivalent fasts: so that he may taste the dire consequences of his offence ... .*"[51] (Qur'ān 5:95)

In this verse three options for restitution have been left open for the offender to choose from: payment in kind out of livestock; feeding the poor; or fasting. It is true that the alternative offerings and punitory payments are there in consideration of the individual's circumstances. However, the important point to note is that all these verses lay down a principle.

Various reasons for the prohibition of hunting during the pilgrimage period have been suggested by commentators. One rational reason which the writer can think of is that, during that period, there is enough meat for all to eat and that the additional meat of game would run to waste. This would, obviously, be against the most important Islamic concept that the killing of animals is sinful, except for the bare necessities of life. For example, in the following verses, the Qur'ān mentions two necessities of life for which cattle may be used:

> "*Of the cattle there are some as beasts of burden and some for meat. Eat of those which Allah has provided for you as sustenance, and follow not the footsteps of the Devil; surely he is your manifest foe.*" (Qur'ān 6:142)

By the 'footsteps of the Devil' is meant, in this context, the then current practice of offering meat to deities and to the misconceived god who was thought to relish the savoury smell of burning flesh and blood. The Qur'ānic injunctions are so exacting on the point of not taking the life of an animal without a justifiable cause (*bighayri ḥaqqin*) that wasting meat, even by offering it to deities and gods is called here a devilish act. Even while allowing Muslims to eat meat, the Qur'ān urges them in remonstrance in verse 6:141 not to waste it by overeating (*Lā tusrifū*). In the following verse this malpractice of wasting meat has been censured more directly and with a touch of sarcasm:

> "*And they set aside as God's share a portion out of the agricultural produce and cattle which God has created, saying fancifully: 'this portion is God's share and that portion is the share of our godlike associates [priests]. In fact the share of the associates never reaches God, while God's share does reach the associates. How ill-conceived is their judgement!*" (Qur'ān 6:136)

A learned Muslim scholar, Shaykh Farīd Wajdī, says in his *Wajdī's Encyclopaedia* – Article on Sacrifice:

> "Islam sanctioned sacrifice and expounded its wisdom and purpose; the wisdom being to induce the rich to spend, the purpose being to

feed the poor unfortunate – for thus said the Lord 'Eat of it and feed the poor unfortunate.'"

Shaykh Wajdī even goes so far as to suggest that there might come a day when Muslims shall have to substitute the rite of animal sacrifice with other methods of giving alms.

An important conference was held in Cairo in 1966 under the auspices of the Academy of Islamic Research in which the famous Muslim scholar, Dr. Maḥmūd Ḥuballāh – the Secretary General of the Academy – and His Eminence The Grand Imām Rector of al-Azhar read their papers.[52] Another member of the Academy, Sheikh 'Abd al-Raḥmān al-Kalḥūd, said in his paper:

"The Holy Qur'ān states in clear terms that the Creator wants the sacrifice not as such but as a symbol of the sacrificer's devotion to God, as is evident from the verse: '*Their flesh will never reach Allah, nor yet their blood, but your devotion will reach Him.*' (Qur'ān 22:37) This verse expressly indicates that the sacrifice is not meant in itself as an essential part of the religion but as an act of charity to enrich the poor.

"At present time, however, sacrificial offerings are thrown away ..., thus defeating the original purpose of *Hady*, namely, to feed the poor and needy. Thus does all this animal wealth run to waste. There is no doubt that this waste is a sort of mischief, '*And Allah*' as the Qur'ān puts it, '*loveth not mischief*. (Qur'ān 2:205)

"It is for this reason that a great number of scholars and reformers have urged that this problem must be solved and a system chalked out to ensure the effective use of sacrificial offerings in the public interest which is supposed to underlie all the ordinances of the canon law."

Another member of the Academy, Shaykh Muḥammad Nūr al-Ḥasan, expressed the following views in his paper:

"Anyone who witnesses the sacrifices slaughtered during the time of pilgrimage, cast away on the ground, unselected by their owners who desist from making them useful to others and afterwards left to decay and putrefy until offensive smell comes out of them, causing the Muslims much discomfort and danger to their health; in short anyone who witnesses the disgraceful state of affairs, will be immensely grieved about Muslims' mismanagement and their unawareness of Islamic rules misleading them to squandering and lavishment regarded as reproved by both Islam and usage. We implore God the Almighty to save Muslims from this ignorance and to guide them to the right path.

"I mention with great regret what aggravates the problem of sacrifices, because a considerable number of pilgrims slaughter their animals and cast them on the ground; they do that thinking that they are offering sacrifices. However, the sacrifice is a *Sunnah*, an example set by the Holy Prophet[(s)] to the resident and not to a newcomer pilgrim as had been stated by Mālik [93-179 A.H. – 673-759 A.C.] who had been the Imām of Madina, the town of the Emigration. If we admit for the sake of a disputed point that it is *Sunnah* for the pilgrim also and that the offering of these sacrifices will certainly lead to disadvantages and misuses, which we witness occurring from them, we ought to give up this harmful usage, because to prevent harmful misuse is prior to seeking benefit deemed to be useful. So, if pilgrims follow Mālik's view as regards sacrifices, they will satisfy themselves and gratify others.

"We pray to God to direct the learned men of every Muslim town and country to enable them to guide their people and to impart to them what is most righteous and advantageous to them in their worldly life and the life to come. I believe that if Muslims conformed with the guidance we have elucidated, they will never face such complications termed as the problem of sacrifices that arise during the season of pilgrimage."

The Conference concluded by passing the following resolution No.4-2:

> "The Conference appeals to all Muslim people and governments to check the dangers which might arise during the pilgrimage from sacrificial offerings, to put them to a good use as is permitted by the Law-giver, to adopt the ways wherewith to accomplish this object."

One could quote many more authorities who have been deploring the Muslim lassitude in solving the problem associated with the senseless killing of animals as sacrifices. Perhaps one more piece of advice by a great scholar might help. Shaykh Ṭanṭāwī Jawharī quotes Ibn Qayyim from his book *Zād al-Maʿād* under the Title: "Legal Rulings Change according to Varying Places, Times and Customs":

> "The canon law is based on wisdom and public interest. It is all justice and all mercy. Any case which changes it from justice to injustice, from mercy to cruelty, from good to evil, from wisdom to nonsense is alien to the common law even if it [the injustice, the cruelty, the evil or the nonsense] has been introduced into it through misinterpretation.
>
> "The [sacrificial gift] *Hady* offered at Minā is meant to achieve a public interest, but in fact, it has involved a harm and a loss of wealth and lives. The chief purpose of that rite is to sustain not to destroy human life. It behoves Muslims to get rid of this disease, ignorance and shame. Indeed it is a folly which Muslims should give up ... Many a solution to this problem may be offered. The most practical one is to preserve the sacrificial offerings and distribute their flesh to the needy."[53]

SACRIFICE BY PROXY

The offering of a sacrifice by proxy for general charity (*Ṣadaqah*, i.e. other than the pilgrimage sacrifice) has always been an established convention among Muslims. People sick in hospitals, or away from home for any other reason, often ask their families to offer a sacrifice in their name and distribute the meat among the poor. It is a common sight in those countries to see a queue of men, women and children at the door of a house where an animal is slaughtered as a sacrifice. Even the skins are donated to charitable organisations.

Many Muslims living in Western countries practise sacrifice by proxy in a similar way as they do for general charity (*Ṣadaqah*). According to the laws in the West, no animal can be slaughtered for trade except under supervision and only in licensed abattoirs. When a Muslim in these countries offers a sacrifice, he or she arranges it with the help of a meat-shop. In the Welfare States of Europe there are hardly any 'poor' to be found. Even if there are some, they often cannot be reached easily. However, the sacrificial meat is consumed by members of the family, friends and neighbours. Muslims in the West are now more inclined either to donate an equivalent amount of cash to some charitable institution or have their sacrifices offered by proxy in their countries of origin.

In order to derive real knowledge and inspiration from the revealed Scriptures, our aim should be to grasp the spirit of the message rather than to give undue devotion to the letter. These discussions on the positive and revealed theology might look to some as pedagogic, but there are millions of people, even in this age of agnosticism and cynicism, who still seek guidance in their respective Scriptures and try to discipline their lives according to their teachings. A misunderstood and misinterpreted doctrine not only defeats its purpose but can sometimes result in harmful consequences. Some Muslim scholars have expressed their concern at the way the Islamic ritual of sacrifice is sometime being interpreted. Allamah Yusuf Ali, the distinguished translator of the Qur'ān says:

> "... the meat then killed is meant to be eaten for food and distributed to the poor and the needy. In present conditions, where much of it is wasted on the spot, it would be a good thing if the surplus meat were canned and utilised for export, or if the sacrifices were performed in some other form approved by due authority."

Then he adds:

> "This is the true end of a sacrifice, not propitiation of higher powers, for God is One, and He does not delight in flesh and blood, but a symbol of thanksgiving to God by sharing meat with fellow-men."[54]

Another distinguished translator of the Qur'ān into English, Muhammad Asad, gives his views as follows:

> "Whereas the pilgrims are merely *permitted* to eat some of the flesh of the animals which they have sacrificed, the feeding of the poor is *mandatory* (Ṭabarī and Zamakhsharī) and constitutes, thus, the primary objective of these sacrifices."[55]

It is generally argued that animal sacrifices during the pilgrimage are 'God's symbols' (*Sha'ā'ir Allāh*), symbolising the worshipper's devotion and gratefulness to God for His bounties to man. This view is based on verses 5:3 and 22:32, 36. What is overlooked, however, is that these verses speak of God's symbols in terms of all the rites of pilgrimage and not exclusively of sacrifices. Many learned scholars, including Ṭabarī, hold the same view. If these verses are studied in their full context, it becomes clear that sacrifice is one of the many other symbols of God and that it becomes a more rewarding symbol of worship if the proviso of charity is fulfilled. Another very important point to note in this respect (verses 22: 34, 35) is that the act of sacrifice becomes a higher symbol of worship when it is done by those who 'submit' (*aslamū*); who do it in 'humility' (*mukhbitīn*); and whose hearts tremble (*wajilat qulūbuhum*) at the time when they are invoking the name of Allah to slaughter an animal, and 'expend on charity out of what We have bestowed on them'

(For the utilisation of the sacrificial meat during *Ḥajj*, see Appendix A at the end of this chapter.)

THE THREE KINDS OF SACRIFICES

The code governing the procedure of pilgrimage does not fall within the preview of this book. There are comprehensive books available on this subject in almost every language. Then there are officially appointed guides (*Mu'allims*) to instruct pilgrims at every step. However, the following brief information is relevant to the subject of pilgrimage sacrifice (*Hady*) and to sacrifice in general:

> There are only three occasions when Muslims offer sacrifice. The first is towards the end of *Ḥajj* when the pilgrims come back to Minā on the tenth of *Dhū'l-Ḥijjah* after staying in 'Arafāt and Muzdalifah. This sacrifice is called *Hady* meaning gifts. In the context of pilgrimage it means the animals offered in sacrifice. The sacrificial animals named in the Qur'ān are of eight kinds of cattle out of three categories, viz. camels, cows or bulls, and sheep or goats.[56] As mentioned earlier, the offerers are allowed to eat of their sacrifices, "but the primary objective is to feed the poor."[57] There is, however, one kind of sacrifice which the pilgrim is not allowed to eat at all and should give the whole sacrifice in charity. This happens if a pilgrim violates any of the prescribed rules during the major pilgrimage, he or she becomes liable to a sort of fine of a special offering called *Dam*.

The rule that the sacrifices must be made within the three days mentioned above has been misunderstood by some Muslims to mean that the meat must be consumed within those three days and that it should not be preserved any longer. There is no authority for this stipulation in any sources of the Islamic law. On the contrary the *Ṣaḥīḥ* of Bukhārī quotes the Holy Prophet[(s)] in *Ḥadīth* 25:124 as having suggested to his Companions, including Jābir ibn 'Abdullāh, to take some left-over sacrificial meat with them as a provision for their journey back. Perhaps this misunderstanding arose originally because of the Biblical rulings limiting the period during which the sacrificial meat could be consumed, the surplus after that period being thrown away.

The second occasion for sacrifice is at the birth of a child, whether male or female, and is called *'Aqīqah*. Putting the female issue on a par with the male might look to be in the natural order of things these days, but in the pre-Islamic period, female infanticide was quite common. The Qur'ān not only stopped the killing of infants after birth, but also gave equal status to both sexes.[58] The birth of a child is a festive occasion for the family and usually friends and the dignitaries of society are invited to a feast. Yet, even on this occasion, the Islamic convention of sacrifice is to share the meat with the poor. Traditionally Muslims distribute the meat into three lots, one for the poor, one for friends and neighbours and one for the family.

The third kind of sacrifice is a pure and simple charity (*Ṣadaqah*). There being no special occasion for it, it is offered by individuals at will as a meritorious act of feeding the poor. Neither the offerer of this sacrifice, nor his or her family or friends have any share in the meat. The skin, as is the case with all sacrifices, is given to some charitable institution. This kind of sacrifice is very common among Muslims all over the world and fulfils a great social need in countries where the normal diet of the poor people lacks food-essentials.

It is significant to note that there is no ritual involved in the sacrificial slaughter. Those Muslims who have started changing this plain matter-of-fact act into a ritual should know better. The two conditions of invoking the name of God and using a sharp knife are the same in sacrificial slaughter as in the normal slaughter for food. The only differentiating stipulation in the case of sacrificial animals is that they should be healthy and free from any perceptible sign of illness. The expression 'free from blemish' is liable to be misunderstood in the Jewish sense of the word 'blemish'. The Islamic definition of 'blemish', according to the Holy Prophet Muḥammad[(s)] is that the sacrificial animal should not be: obviously diseased; raw-boned lean; blind even in one eye; or lame.[59] With the exception of a diseased animal, which people do not eat anyway, the other three are the only additional conditions laid down for sacrificial animals. One plausible reason for these additional conditions is to make sure that the poor people for whom these sacrifices are offered get reasonably good quality meat.

APPENDIX A

The following letter from the Islamic Development Bank, Jeddah, Saudi Arabia, dated August 1986, is self-explanatory:

"To: Al-Hafiz B.A.Masri ...,

Dear Sir,

The Government of the Kingdom of Saudi Arabia, keeping in view the wastage of meat during Eid Al-Adha, has established a Sacrificial Meat Utilization Project in 1983 on an experimental basis and devoted particular attention to this project as it does regarding all matters related to the Hajj.

Following several studies carried out by the concerned authorities in the Kingdom of Saudi Arabia regarding the optimal use of the sacrificial meat, a special committee has been set up to supervise the implementation of the project. The committee includes the Islamic Development Bank (IDB), which co-operates with the Saudi competent authorities.

The first experiment took place in the 1403H. [1983 A.C.] Hajj season. The meat of 63,000 heads was utilised, most of which was airlifted to refugees in Sudan, Djibouti and to Afghan refugees in Pakistan. For purposes of the project, the al-Moaisim Slaughterhouse was designed by the Saudi Government and fully equipped with the most modern installations.

In the light of the first year's experience, it was decided to expand the project. In 1404H. [1984 A.C.] Hajj season, the meat of 186,195 heads of sheep was utilised, of which about 144,000 heads were airlifted and distributed to the poor Muslim communities in Djibouti, Bangladesh, Chad, Yemen Arab Republic, as well as to Afghan refugees in Pakistan and Palestinian refugees in Jordan, besides what was distributed at Al-Haram.

In the light of the project's success in 1403H. and 1404H., thanks be to Allah, it was envisaged to expand the project in 1405H. Hajj season. The programme for the 1405 H. Hajj season aimed at utilising 300,000 heads of sheep, but due to the growing response and support which the project received from the pilgrims, the number of coupons sold exceeded the target figure by over 7,000.

In 1405H. a complete unit with all necessary equipment was added to the Al-Moaisim Slaughterhouse to make use of some of the offals of the sacrificed animals. Moreover, two cold rooms, each with a capacity of 50,000 heads, were added for freezing the meat.

The expansion in the programme can be gauged from the fact that in its first year, i.e. 1403., 63,000 sheep were utilised. In the second year (1404H.) the number of sheep utilised was 186,195 and the number in 1405H. was 307,266.

In 1406H. [1986 A.C.], 350,000 sheep have been utilised and the meat has been distributed on the same lines as in 1405H. in Sudan, Pakistan, Djibouti, Bangladesh, Jordan, Chad, Yemen (DR), Mauritania, Mali, Burkina Faso, Egypt, Senegal, Gambia, Syria and Niger.

The Muna Development Office is presently preparing studies on the financial allocation required for the second model slaughterhouse.

When the second slaughterhouse is completed, the project will be extended to include camels and cattle as well as sheep. It is intended in future years also to utilise the parts of the slaughtered animals other than their meat.

As far as sacrifices by proxy are concerned, I would like to inform you that there is no objection to the authorisation of slaughtering the animals. The upright Islamic Shariah allows the Muslim, in carrying out the slaughtering of his sacrificial offering, to authorise whoever he deems as a trustworthy representative. The representative is expected to fulfil such authorisation in accordance with the requirements of the Shariah. You in turn should fully observe these requirements. Any offering given as an atonement for committing a prohibition or as a reparation for failing to observe a required duty must be distributed to the poor in Makkah. As for any other type of sacrificial offering, the meat can be distributed to the poor in Makkah or to other pilgrims or to anyone else as provided by the Shari'ah. Hoping that this can meet your requirements as mentioned in your letter.

Best regards.

Yours faithfully,
(Abdul Fattah Kiswani)
Head: Sacrificial Meat Office

The Government of the Kingdom of Saudi Arabia deserve felicitations on their resolution to solve this problem. Let us hope that soon their efforts will succeed in the utilisation of every ounce of meat and the by-products of every sacrificial animal for the purpose of charity for which the institution of animal sacrifice was originally established by Islam.

REFERENCES AND NOTES

1. cf. *The Way of Heaven*; Taylor, R. L.; E.J. Brill, Leiden; 1985.
2. *Lun-Yu*, 3:17, as recorded in *The Analects of Confucius;* Arthur Waley; Vintage, New York; 1938; p.98.
3. *Lun-Yu*, 7:1, as recorded in *Sources of Chinese Tradition*; S. J. de Bary; Columbia University Press, New York; 1960; p.25.
4. *Yogasastra*, 11:39.
5. cf. *The Bodhisattva Doctrine in Buddhist Sanskrit Literature*; Har Dayal; Kegan Paul & Co., London; 1931; also cf. *Avadana Kalpalata.*
6. *The Epistle of St. Paul the apostle to the Romans, 8:22, 23.*
7. *Isa.* 45:1.
8. *Joel.* 3:9-17.
9. *Exod.* 29:40.
10. *Deut.* 12:20-28.
11. *Lev.* 3:11; 21:21; *Num.* 28:2.
12. *Ezek.* 44:16. *Malachi*, 1:7.
13. *Lev.* 6:16; 7:6.
14. *Gen.* 8:20, 21.
15. *Talmud* is the body of Jewish civil and canonical law, consisting of *Mishna* and *Gemara.* The final version was completed in the 5th century. *Midrash* is the haggadic scriptural exegesis, especially that which was made during a period of about 1,800 years after Exile. *Targums* (Hebrew: *Targumim*; Arabic: *Tarājim*) are the translations of some portions of the Old Testament in Aramaic Judea.
16. For full details of the Cabalist concept see: *Zohar; Sefer ha-Bahir; Issac the Blind; Egra;* and *Azriel of Gerona.*
17. *Lev.* 16:20-22; 4:20; 5:10.
18. *Lev.* 16:8.
19. *Gen.* 4:3-5.
20. *Gen.* 8:20, 21.

21. *Job.* 1:1-5.
22. *Job.* 42:7, 8.
23. *Gen.* 31:45-54.
24. *Gen.* 46:1.
25. *Gen.* 12:7, 8; 13:3, 4.
26. *Gen.* 22:13.
27. *Gen.* 26:25.
28. *Gen.* 33:20; 35:7.
29. For details see: *Leviticus, Numbers, II Kings.*
30. *Lev.* 12:6-8; 15:14, 15, 29, 30; 16:3, 5, 24. *Exod.* 29:38-42. *Num.* 6:10, 11, 14-16; 28:1-14, 19-29; 29:2-4, 8, 12-38.
31. *Isaiah*, 1:11-15.
32. *Hosea*, 6:4-6.
33. *Amos*, 5:18-22.
34. *Psalm of Asaph*, 50:7-14.
35. *Jer.* 7:21.
36. Moses ben Maimun, the famous Spanish Jewish Rabbi, philosopher and writer (1135-1204 A.C.).
37. *Ber.* 4:1; 7:266.
38. *Hertz Prayer Book*; Joseph Hertz; 15:7. Also cf. 33, 34.
39. *The Jewish Religion*; Michael Friedlander; 1913; p.417.
40. *Facts and Fallacies About Liberal Judaism*; originally by Rabbi Hooker, revised by Sidney Brichto, London; 1972; p.14.
41. A general tribunal, called the Holy Office, was developed by the Roman Catholic Church under Pope Innocent III and Pope Gregory IX (1198-1241) to make inquisitional examination of the so-called heretics. The Spanish Inquisition has gone down in history as the most torturous of them all, during the 15th and the 16th centuries. The Inquisition was abolished in France in 1772 and in Spain in 1834.
42. *Joshua.* 9:21.
43. *War – Living Graves*; Shaw, George Bernard; Irish dramatist and scholar; (1856 – 1950).
44. The Qur'ān: 4:164; 10:47; 13:7; 16:36; 35:24; 40:78.
45. The Qur'ān: 4:150, 151.
46. There are numerous passages in the Qur'ān about Prophet Abraham(s) and Jesus Christ(s). The following few references will give a general idea: About Abraham: 2:124, 130; 3:33; 16:120; 21:69; 22:78; 38:45-47. About Christ: 4:171; 43:57; 61:14.

47. cf. *Encyclopaedia Britannica* – Article on Sacrifice. Also cf. *The Origins of Sacrifice;* James, E. O.; pp. 84-86.
48. cf. *The Religion of the Semites*; Robertson Smith. Also cf. *Encyclopedia of Religion and Ethics*; Hastings.
49. cf. *Ibn Kathīr*; Vol III; p.221.
50. The Qur'ān, 2:196; 22:28, 35-37.
51. The Qur'ān, 5:98. Also cf. 5:2, 97.
52. The Third Conference of the Academy of Islamic Research; G.O. Government Printing Offices, Cairo, 13810-1966-3,000 ex., 1966; pp. 115-130.
53. Shaykh Ṭanṭāwī Jawharī in his book entitled *Al-Jawāhir*, as a Commentary on Chapter 22 of the Qur'ān.
54. *The Holy Qur'ān*; A. Yusuf Ali; Sh.Muhammad Ashraf, Kashmiri Bazar, Lahore, Pakistan; footnotes Nos. 2802 and 2810 to verses 22:28, 34.
55. *The Message of the Qur'ān*; Muhammad Asad; Dar al-Andalus, Gibraltar; footnote No. 42 to verse 22:28.
56. The Qur'ān, 6:143. Also cf. *Bidāyat al-Mujtahid* of Ibn Rushd.
57. cf. Ṭabarī and Zamakhsharī.
58. The Qur'ān, 6:151; 17:31.
59. *Al-Muwaṭṭa'* of Imām Mālik on the authority of al-Barā' ibn 'Āzib.

CHAPTER FOUR

ḤALĀL MEAT
THE BONE OF CONTENTION

Preamble

SOME LIGHT HAS been thrown in previous chapters on the emphasis which Islam lays on an all-embracing relationship with the environment – each creature and element working as a coefficient agent of nature. All species of sentient beings are covenanted to be complementary in the utilisation of each other's intrinsic potentialities. Those who take undue advantage of other species break the Divine Law of equilibrium in nature – and nature never forgives. The Qur'ān dwells on this theme recurrently, such as:

> "*Allah has not created all this without truth* [Ḥaqq] (Qur'ān 10:5); *for it is He Who created everything, and ordained it with due potential* [Taqdīr]" (Qur'ān 25:2); *"not to allow any change to corrupt what Allah has created"* (Qur'ān 30:30)

Then a warning is given to those people who are guilty of infraction, in these words:

> *"Do they not know how many We have annihilated before them – those whom We had established on earth as more powerful than We have established you ...*" (Qur'ān 6:6).

Anyone who tries to understand the Islamic teachings on this subject will find that, even in his relentless search for food, man has to keep himself within the bounds of humanity, compassion and mercy so as not to cause any unnecessary and avoidable pain to the victims of his needs. Muslims generally know what is *Ḥalāl* and *Ḥarām*. They also have a general idea about the method of slaughter as prescribed by Islam. However, it cannot be denied that there does exist some confusion in matters of detail among some Muslims. This is mostly due to the fact that the various aspects of the Islamic dietary laws are presented to the Muslim public as isolated and incohesive excerpts from the Qur'ān and *Aḥādīth*. This sketchy information does not help laymen to sort out their priorities in a given situation.

An overall study of the law leaves no doubt that Islam does not want us to be uncompromisingly austere in our dietetic regimen. It does not want us to end up like the orthodox Hindus who would throw away their food if it gets even touched by a non-Hindu. Mahatma Gandhi's clan strongly opposed his parents' decision to send him to England for education on the grounds that the child would lose caste by crossing the waters and eating non-Hindu food. Orthodox Jews have imposed on themselves segregation by their over-exacting laws of diet. However, the writer has come across quite a few Muslims who would not eat even at other Muslims' houses because they are not prepared to take on trust the orthodoxy of the host. This has started happening to the followers of the Prophet(s) who repeatedly emphasised the socio-cultural importance of mutual exchange of hospitality. For example, he says:

> "Eat in company, not alone, for congregation inspires Divine Grace", or "One who is invited to a meal and does not respond, gives offence to Allah and His Messenger."

Those living in Islamic countries have little idea of the dietary problems which Muslims in the West have to face. During the past few decades millions of Muslims have migrated to Western countries. Until a few years ago, *Ḥalāl* meat shops were few and far between. Even these days people have to travel long distances in some areas to get *Ḥalāl* meat.

An attempt has been made in this chapter to discuss some problems which are confronting the oncoming Muslim generations in their daily lives. Questions such as the lawfulness or unlawfulness (*Ḥalāl* or *Ḥarām*) of meat slaughtered by Christians and Jews and the question of pre-slaughter stunning, are not only important from the theological point of view but they have also become emotive ethnological issues. The purpose of this discussion is to present bare facts in the light of Islamic teachings, leaving the inference to the reader's judgement. However, the writer has availed himself of the liberty of conscience to express his personal views on some of the controversial issues, in the hope that readers would find them helpful. After all, the new generations of Muslims are to live all their lives in countries of non-Islamic culture and religion. Not only they, but in time all their succeeding generations too, will have to live in similar situations. They will be able to keep up their heritage not by shutting themselves up in their own cultural ghettos but by an educated sense of compatibility and integration – as opposed to assimilation.

LAWFUL AND UNLAWFUL MEAT

The Qur'ān has laid down general guidance about what kind of animals are lawful (*Ḥalāl*) or unlawful (*Ḥarām*) to eat, while *Aḥādīth* and the jurists (*Fuqahā'*) have elucidated those laws. The important point to note in this respect is that the prohibition of certain foods is solely for hygienic reasons. Keeping in mind the long-term influences of diet on the consumer's ethos, the dietetic laws are meant to be taken seriously, albeit not so seriously as to jeopardize one's very health or life. That is why all restrictions are lifted in circumstances of genuine need and distress. Summarily the following animals are lawful as food in Islam:

The cud-chewing animals (ruminants) such as cattle, sheep, goats, camels, buffaloes, wild ruminants; animals which live permanently in water (aquatics) such as fish and members of the mammalian order (cetaceans) such as whales; and most birds. It is taken for granted that every species of animal and bird is permissible as food unless specifically prohibited in the Qur'ān or *Ḥadīth*. Some of them so named are: pigs; some of those living both on land and in water, though not able to breathe under water (amphibia) such as frogs and crocodiles; all the flesh-eating mammalia (carnivores) – whether domesticated or wild – such as cats, dogs, wolves, jackals, foxes, lions, tigers; animals which are zoologically human in form (anthropoids or simiods) such as monkeys and apes; most of the creeping creatures (reptiles and amoeba) such as snakes and toxic lizards; animals feeding on carrion or refuse (scavengers) and birds that prey with their claws or talons such as kites, crows, eagles and hawks. Asses, donkeys and mules are prohibited, but there is a difference of opinion about wild asses, zebras and quaggas. Blood is prohibited, but only that which pours forth at the time of slaughter. (Qur'ān 6:145). That which is left in the body as residuum is washed off before cooking.[1]

THE QUR'ĀNIC DIETARY ORDINANCES

It is noteworthy that the four Schools of Thought in Islam, mistakenly called 'sects' by some, are agreed on the quintessence of Islamic dietary laws, except on some points of detail.[2]

The Qur'ān speaks of 'sin' not only in terms of dereliction of moral rectitude, but also in the sense of violation of the physical laws of nature. All its dietary laws are based on the principle that both the physical and the metaphysical existence of man are inversely correspondent. Those who seek to interpret these laws as merely ritualistic symbols benefit from them neither spiritually nor physically. These days the real problem in understanding the true spirit of those laws is that most of the classical literature on this subject was written some centuries ago, when human lifestyles and its contingencies were different. What is needed now is the reappraisal and reinterpretation of those laws – of course within the bounds of the Divine code (*Sharī'ah*) – to keep religion a dynamic force. There are quite a few verses laying down the law on food, which will be discussed later. First, it is important to discuss the following verse which is the most comprehensive of them all:

> "*Forbidden to you is that which dies of itself; blood; flesh of swine; that on which any name other than that of Allah has been invoked; the strangled animals; that beaten to death; that killed by a fall; that gorged to death with the horn; that [parts of] which wild beasts have eaten – except those which you [are able to] slaughter; that which is sacrificed on stones set up [as idols]; and that on which you draw lots by arrows. This day have I perfected your religion for you .... However, if one is compelled by hunger – not inclining wilfully to sin – then surely Allah is Forgiving, Merciful.*" (Qur'ān 5:3)

A careful analysis of this verse shows that the prohibited food falls into four categories, viz. carrion, blood, pork, and animals killed idolatrously. A further analysis shows that the prohibition is based on two considerations, viz. physical as well as metaphysical welfare. Pork, blood, or the flesh of animals which are dead (*Maytah*) for any reason before being cleansed of blood (*Tadhkiyah*) are physically unhealthy (*Rijs*) to eat. Animals killed idolatrously or even heretically – such as sortition by arrows – are detrimental to spiritual health (*Fisq*). However, here again, Islam qualifies this law with reservations for exceptional circumstances. The extenuatory clause at the end of the verse applies to everything listed as unlawful (*Ḥarām*).

"Animals slaughtered on stones" refers to the stone altars on which sacrifices used to be offered to deities and idols by pagans.[3] "The drawing of lots by arrows" refers to the pagan practice of portioning out the sacrificial meat among themselves by shooting flat and featherless arrows (*al-azlām*) at them.[4] This verse was revealed to the Holy Prophet Muḥammad[(s)] 81 or 82 days before his death, which makes it the final word on the Qur'ānic dietary law.[5]

Another significant point to note in this verse is that all injured animals – such as those mutilated by wild beasts and partly eaten by them, beaten up, strangulated or gorged – are allowed to be eaten provided they are live enough to be bled.[6] This Qur'ānic ruling is of great significance in relation to the Jewish objection to causing an injury and a blemish to the animal by stunning it before slaughter. The Islamic approach in this respect is in sharp contrast to that of Judaism. The Islamic prohibition imposed on all the above categories of animals is abrogated *ipso facto* in cases where they can be bled by slaughter – irrespective of the extent, nature or cause of their injuries. The point cannot be over-emphasised that the Islamic dietetic law is based on the utility value of all the resources of food in general and of food-animals in particular. The very survival of a living being depends on nutriment. That is why even pork has been allowed to be eaten in case of exigency, with the qualifying clauses of not relishing it (*ghayra bāghin*) nor consuming more than necessary (*wa lā 'ādin*).

The Islamic juristic rule is: "what is not declared as unlawful is lawful." The Qur'ān repeatedly upbraids the fanatical zealots who add their own pedantic doctrinaire to the straightforward Divine Law. It criticises those who take their theologians as gods in Chapter 9, verse 31. When requested by a Companion named 'Adiyy ibn Ḥātim to explain, the Holy Prophet[(s)] replied that such people declare some lawful things as unlawful and some unlawful things as lawful and thus act as if they were the Lords (*Arbāb*). The pith of the Qur'ānic message in this respect is not to impose on oneself unnecessary abstinence and to thankfully enjoy all the good and pure bounties (*ṭayyibāt*) of nature. The following few verses will serve as an example, and would perhaps help Muslim readers in resolving some of their dietetic problems in the West:

> "*O messengers! eat of the good things* [ṭayyibāt] *and do righteous deeds. Surely, I know what you do.*" (Qur'ān 23:51)

> "*O believers! eat what We have provided for you of lawful and good things, and give thanks for Allah's favour, if it is He whom you serve.*" (Qur'ān 2:172; 16:114)

The word '*Ṭayyib*', translated as 'good', 'pure', 'wholesome', etc. has already been explained to mean pure both in the physical and the moral sense. For example, food obtained by any illegal or unethical means, such as by subjecting the animals to cruelties in their breeding, transport, slaughter, or in their general welfare, cannot be regarded as wholesome

"*... He [Muḥammad] enjoins them to good and forbids them evil and makes lawful to them the good things and prohibits for them impure things, and removes from them their burden and the shackles which used to be on them...*" (Qur'ān 7:157).

"*Say [O Muḥammad!] I find not in what has been revealed to me any food [meat] forbidden to those who wish to eat it, unless it be dead meat, or blood that pours forth, or the flesh of swine – for it is unclean* [rijs] *– or the sacrilegious* [fisq] *meat which has been slaughtered in anybody's name other than that of Allah. However, if one is stressed by necessity [one may eat any of the above mentioned things] without wilful disobedience and without transgressing the due limits. [In that case, know that] thy Lord is Forgiving and Merciful.*" (Qur'ān 6:145)

The message of the above verse is repeated in other verses to lay stress upon the point that it is only those categories of food which have been named which are unlawful to eat and that the rest is lawful, (Qur'ān 2:173; 16:115). The reason for this repetition and emphasis seems to have been to liberate Muslims from the then prevalent pre-Islamic interdicts on food, most of which were superstitious and superfluous.

The Qur'ān puts a question in these words:

"*And what reason have you that you should not eat of that on which Allah's name has been pronounced, when He has already explained to you in detail what is forbidden – excepting that which you are compelled to eat under necessity? Yet there are those who lead people astray by their low desires out of ignorance. Surely your Lord – He knows the transgressors.*" (Qur'ān 6:119)

"*Of the cattle there are some for burden and some for slaughter as food. Eat what Allah has provided for you as sustenance, and do not be led by the devil – he is your manifest foe.*" (Qur'ān 6:142)

By the devil in this context is meant those who take the law into their own hands by declaring lawful things as unlawful and *vice versa*. Arbitrary taboos in religion make its laws unconformable and the life of its followers unnecessarily difficult.

The Qur'ān declares the final judgement in these words:

"*Today [all] things good and pure have been made lawful for you ...*" (Qur'ān 5:3).

The general counsel of the Qur'ān regarding food is of moderation in eating and of a well-balanced discernment between the lawful and the unlawful. Out of many verses on this theme, the following would suffice here:

"*O believers! make not unlawful the good things which Allah has made lawful for you, and exceed not the limits – for Allah does not hold dear those who overpass the limits.*" (Qur'ān 5:87)

Many commentators have elucidated the Qur'ānic wording *Lā-ta'tadū* (do not exceed the limits) and *Lā tuḥarrimū* (do not declare as forbidden). It is generally agreed that the injunction 'do not exceed the limits' means that one should not indulge in gluttony. However, the counterpart of the true sense often remains unappreciated that this injunction also qualifies the preceding injunction of 'do not declare as forbidden' and therefore can be taken to mean:

'do not exceed the limitations by declaring lawful things as unlawful'. In this context the latter interpretation is more in accord with the general drift of this and other verses on this theme. The next verse further supports this interpretation by laying stress on the counsel to eat of all good and pure things. Some illustrious authorities, such as Zamakhsharī, Ṭabarī, and Rāzī, opine that these verses are meant to dissuade people from the monastic tendencies of self-mortification by denying themselves legitimate creature comforts and by unnecessary abstinence from good food.

FOOD OF THE "PEOPLE OF THE BOOK"

The verse 5:5, while declaring all good and pure things as lawful to eat, continues to declare:

> " ...*And the food of those who have been given the Book is lawful for you and your food is lawful for them...*"

The learned commentators believe that the Arabic word *Ṭa'ām* used for food means 'meat' in this context. According to 'Abdullāh ibn 'Abbās, who was a Companion of the Holy Prophet(s), *Ṭa'ām* here means slaughtered meat (*Dhabīhah*).[7]

By the "People of the Book" is meant the followers of those scriptures which are historically acknowledged to have been revealed by God. Muslims generally apply this term (*Ahl al-Kitāb* or *Kitābī*) to Christians and Jews. However, during the early days of Islam, the Persians also were included. Originally Sabians too were included in this term, but this religion does not exist any more.[8]

It is a latent condition in this verse that only that kind of the *Kitābīs'* food which is permissible to Muslims is that which is lawful (*Ḥalāl*) according to Islamic law. Until recently the question whether or not the meat slaughtered by Christians was lawful used to be more or less of academic interest. These days, however, it has started posing itself with all its pragmatical implications. Although the above verse puts the Christians and the Jews in the same bracket, many Muslims have been feeling an aversion to Christian food since the time when St. Paul declared the flesh of swine as lawful. For Muslims leading a quiet and religiously conventional life within Islamic countries, the question does not warrant a serious discussion. However, for Muslims living in Christian countries it affects not only their daily diet but also their social life and has to be thrashed out.

THE PARADOXICAL ENIGMA OF PORK

It is generally argued that, at the time when the above-quoted verse (5:5) was revealed, Christians used to observe the Mosaic prohibition of swine-flesh; which they no longer do. However, this line of reasoning is based on the false premise that, while revealing this verse, Allah did not know that there would come a time when Christians and Jews would start to ignore some of the Biblical dietetic laws. According to Muslim credence Allah is All-Knowing; His knowledge is above the limitations of time and space. Surely, His knowledge did comprehend all this. Had it been within the design of His wisdom to allow Muslims to eat the meat slaughtered by the *Kitābīs* as a transient expediency, He would have put in some sort of a caveat in this verse to the effect that Muslims should stop eating meat slaughtered by them when they started eating pork. It is not the Muslims' concern what Christians and Jews eat. They should be concerned only to the extent that they themselves do not eat those items of their food which have been specifically named as forbidden by the Islamic law (*Sharī'ah*) and that they should not impose on themselves any restrictions beyond that. The famous Kūfī theologian – al-Sha'bī (d.722 A.C.), while commenting on this verse, says that Allah knows what the *Kitābīs* do and it is He who allowed us to eat meat slaughtered by them.

It is imperative to keep in mind throughout this discourse, the ruling (*Fatwā*) of the Imāms Abū Ḥanīfah and Ibn Ḥanbal.[9] According to them the

Qur'ānic permission to Muslims to eat the food (meat) of the People of the Book is restricted to those things which have been declared as lawful. Things declared as unlawful for Muslims are not to be eaten in any case. The opinions of Muslim authorities, quoted below, take for granted this postulate:

> One of the early authorities to pronounce an edict (*Fatwā*) on this issue was Ma'bad al-Juhanī (d.660 A.C., 80 A.H.). According to him, meat slaughtered by Christians is lawful for Muslims. 'Aṭā' ibn Yasār (d.721 A.C.) who was the Judge (*Qāḍī*) of Madina, endorsed his views. Similarly, al-Layth and Rabī'ah (both d. 791 A.C.) have expressed their verdicts to the same effect.[10] Sayyid Sābiq also adds in *Fiqh al-Sunnah* that meat slaughtered by Christians and Jews is lawful.[11] Sarakhsī (d. 899 A.C.) even went so far as to say: "the flesh of an animal slaughtered by a Christian or a Jew is ALWAYS lawful for Muslims to eat … .[12] It is significant to note that such edicts started being issued within a few years after the death of the Holy Prophet[(s)] when there were many learned authorities still alive who had direct knowledge of the Holy Prophet's[(s)] sayings and deeds, and yet none of the Muslims contradicted these verdicts. Below are the edicts of some very prominent succeeding theologians: "The first and *prima facie* view is that their (*Kitābīs*') foods are lawful for the Muslims …"[13]
>
> The Muftī of Jordan says:
>
> "The jurists have agreed that a Muslim is allowed to eat meat offered by a man of the People of the Book. It is not right for him to suspect the method of their slaughtering and whether or not the name of God has been invoked at the time of slaughtering. It is not even good to make an enquiry on the subject, because the verses in the Qur'ān are absolute without any restrictions (*Muṭlaq*). A considerable number of religious doctors have said that animals cut by a man of the 'People of the Book'

> are permitted for Muslims to eat, whatever may be the method of slaughtering.
>
> "Those who do not eat their meat in Europe and U.S.A., according to opinions held by some who are against the above-mentioned opinion, have no reason for doing so, save illusion (*wahm*). This opinion [supporting the prohibition of the Jewish or Christian-slaughtered meat] goes against the majority view, which allows meat cut by Christians and Jews for Muslims."[14]

Maulana Sa'id Ahmad Akbarabadi, the celebrated Muslim theologian of India, has endorsed the views of the Mufti of Jordan.[15]

An eminent Egyptian scholar and theologian, Khallāf, says:

> "The cattle and all other animals which the Christians and Jews slaughter in a manner which makes it lawful for them to eat according to their religions, are lawful for Muslims to eat."[16]

Another prominent Muslim scholar, al-'Abbādī, bases his views on the Qur'ān 5:6 to say that the most important point is whether or not the slaughter has been carried out in accordance with religious prescript, and that it makes no difference whether or not the slaughterer is a Muslim or one from among the People of the Book.[17]

The following Muslim scholars of great authority have opined that, according to the Qur'ānic verse 5:6, the meat sold in Christian and Jewish shops in the West is lawful for Muslims: (1) Shaykh Muḥammad 'Abduh, former Muftī of Egypt. (2) Shaykh Rashīd Riḍā, a student of Shaykh Muḥammad 'Abduh. (3) Shaykh Maḥmūd Shaltūt, former Rector of al-Azhar. (4) Dr. Yūsuf al-Qaraḍāwī of Qatar.

The verdict of another authority from Jordan, al-Khayyāṭ, is that such meats are lawful for Muslims and that;

> "we are not required to consider the way in which animals have been slaughtered, and whether or not Allah's name has been mentioned on them ... Foodstuffs imported from countries of the People of the Book are lawful unless there is evidence that they are unlawful for themselves, such as carrion, blood or swine-flesh."[18]

The Director of Islamic affairs, Qatar, also agreed with the above verdicts. The great Indian Muslim educationalist and commentator of the Qur'ān, Sir Sayyid Aḥmad Khān (d. 1898 A.C.), was on his way to London and ate the meat provided on the ship. He says in one of his letters describing his voyage:

> "After an inquiry we came to know that the process of slaughtering animals, such as sheep and lambs is to cut their jugular veins with a sharp knife – for their blood is unlawful to Christians .... The meat is, according to our religion, lawful for Muslims."[19]

Thousands of Muslim businessmen, diplomats, tourists and professional people travel to Western countries every day and stay in hotels where they eat meat supplied by Christian butchers. Many such dignitaries are personally known to the writer as good practising Muslims. They instruct the Management not to serve them any food which contains swine-flesh or lard, and their wishes are complied with. Many of the Islamic organisations in the West are dependent for their very existence on the donations from such so-called unorthodox Muslims. However, in the light of the following incident recorded in *Ḥadīth*, they are not guilty of violation of any Islamic law in eating meat in Western hotels:

> "Some Companions of the Holy Prophet Muḥammad[(s)], during their travels in Syria, ate the meat supplied by Christians without enquiring as to how the animals were slaughtered." An Islamic Magazine of Geneva has also supported this conclusion.[20]

IS JEWISH FOOD *ḤALĀL*?

Some Muslim theologians have recently started advising that the meat slaughtered only by orthodox Jews is lawful. This poses the unsolvable problem of ascertaining who is or is not an orthodox Jew. Once such a principle is accepted, there is no reason why it should not apply to the Muslim slaughtermen as well. What it amounts to in practical terms is that a customer should ask at the *Ḥalāl* and *Kosher* shops, before buying the meat, whether or not the animal was slaughtered by a practising orthodox Muslim or Jew. One wonders what would be the advice of such theologians if the shop-owner says that he does not know. People who bandy such pieces of advice succeed only in making religious discipline insufferable and act against the spirit of the Qur'ānic axiom that religious discipline should be easy to follow and not a source of hardship. (Qur'ān 2:185) Again the Qur'ān declares this maxim in these words:

> " *... Allah does not desire to make [religious discipline] any impediment to you; but He does desire to purify you ...*" (Qur'ān 5:6).

Those Muslim theologians (*'Ulamā'*) who recommend *Kosher* meat as *Ḥalāl*, while the Christian-slaughtered meat as *Ḥarām* should make their assurance doubly sure in the light of the following statements by independent authorities:

> "A high proportion of Shechita meat which has been rejected by the Jewish Inspectors as being non-Kosher [*Ḥarām*] is therefore distributed to the open market."[21]

Most poultry going for religious slaughter comes from the spent hen trade [hens which have stopped laying eggs]" ... "For Shechita slaughter, only those birds which are completely healthy and good specimens are selected. This selection is often carried out on the lorry before the crated birds are off-loaded. We have seen such a practice and noted in this instance that those birds which the handler considered unsuitable for Shechita slaughter were re-crated for despatch to other outlets such as street markets [and Muslim shops]" ... "We found that on retail premises where slaughter of poultry is carried out by the Muslim method, live birds (some of which are 'rejects' for Shechita slaughter) are kept in crates or pens ..."[22]

"It has been drawn to our attention that animals (particularly poultry) are being slaughtered by religious methods when it is known at the time of slaughter that the meat is to be sold on to the alternative markets."[23]

BLOOD

It has now been scientifically established that blood contains toxic substances which the body discharges through urine, after being filtered in the kidneys. From the Islamic point of view, it is a symbol of life only in the sense that it supplies nutrients to the tissue-cells.

The Qur'ān has very judiciously circumscribed the prohibition only to that blood which flows out of the body after slaughter (*daman masfūḥan*). (Qur'ān. 6:145) By this qualification, Islam has freed the Muslims from the practice of removing every particle of blood from the flesh in order to make it *Kosher* or *Ḥalāl*. The reason for this liberality in the law is that Islam rejects the concept of any symbolic sacredness of blood. It is to be considered of paramount importance only because it keeps a body alive – and all life is to be considered as sacrosanct. Otherwise, Islam attaches no sacrificial or mysterious significance to it. Islam's prohibition of blood is solely on the grounds of hygiene. Muslims generally wash and rinse the meat before cooking and take it for granted that the residual particles on the flesh would be neutralised by the heat of cooking.

THE INVOCATION OF GOD'S NAME (*TASMIYAH* AND *TAKBĪR*)

Islam has laid down two covenants on the act of slaughter in order to make the meat permissible to eat (*Ḥalāl*). One is the covenant regarding the method of slaughtering and cleansing the carcass (*dhabḥ* and *tadhkiyah*). The second covenant of invoking the name of God at slaughter is often confused with the Jewish ritual of slaughter. This invocation consists of a short sentence comprising two pithy phrases; viz. *Bismillāh*, meaning "in the name of God" and is called *tasmiyah*, i.e. "to call the name". The second phrase is *Allāhu Akbar*, meaning "God is the Greatest" and is called *takbīr*, i.e. "the glorification of God". No other prayer or supplication is required to be added to the wording: "*Bismillāh, Allāhu Akbar*". There is no authority to support the mistaken impression of some Muslims that it should be uttered more than once at each slaughter. It seems that some pietistical Muslim butchers have given a wrong impression to a prominent writer about the Islamic law of slaughter. He says: "As the Muslim ritual requires that, during the ceremony, a prayer must be repeated three times, some Muslims apparently think that the throat should be severed in three stages as opposed to the rapid single, to and fro, movement of the Jews."[24]

Takbīr is meant to be much more than a mere ritual. In view of the sanctity Islam attaches to life, the invocation of God's name at the time of slaughtering an animal is meant to remind the slaughterer that:

He has no right to take this life without Allah's permission; that, except for Allah's permission, the meat of this animal would have been unlawful (*Ḥarām*) for him to eat; that a Muslim accepts the authority of no god other than of One God who is the Greatest Authority; that he thanks Allah for making it lawful for him to use animals for his sustenance; and that the act of slaughter should be performed in a spirit of humility with a trembling heart at the mention of God's name.

Marmaduke Pickthall explains the significance of *Takbīr* at slaughter in his commentary on these verses in these words:

> "In order that they may realise the awfulness of taking life, and the solemn nature of the trust which Allah has imposed on them in the permission to eat animal food."[25]

Killing a living being is after all an act of iniquity. Those who feel justified in killing animals for food are expected to remind themselves at the time of cutting each throat that God is the only One (*Wāḥid*) authority Who can grant dispensation from the penalty of this iniquitous act. The glorification of God's name (*takbīr*) is meant to be an avowal of that Authority as well as a benediction by way of thankfulness to God. The real spirit and sentiment of God's glorification at the time of slaughter remains an expression of thankfulness to Him only if the remains of the slaughtered animal are put to the use for which God has granted the dispensation and are not wasted. Any waste amounts to ungratefulness of His bounty; and the invocation of any other god, deity, idol or patron saint (*Walī*) makes a mockery of God's Authority – the one and only God who is the Creator (*Khāliq*) and the Owner (*Mālik*) of that animal. Human beings in general and Muslims in particular must realise that, in the eyes of the Creator, an animal is worth much more than its weight in flesh.

Taking the teachings of Islam on this subject in their entirety leaves one with the impression that the Islamic Law lays much greater emphasis on the invocation of *Takbīr* than on the method of slaughter (*Dhabḥ*). The following verses of the Qur'ān and *Aḥādīth* establish the fact that, under certain circumstances, the meat of an animal becomes lawful to eat (*Ḥalāl*), even if its blood has not been drawn out by slaughter – but the stipulation of *Takbīr* stands in all circumstances. Apparently, the issue seems to be plain enough not to need any involved discussion. However, there are certain details on which Muslim savants are not unanimous. One serious point of concern in this respect for Muslims in the West is whether or not meat slaughtered by Christians is lawful. The Qur'ānic approbation of their meat has been mentioned earlier. (Qur'ān 5:5) In spite of this, the objectors give three main reasons for rejecting Christian-slaughtered meat. The question of pork has already been discussed. The second reason is the Christian method of slaughter in general and use of stunners. The third reason, which concerns us here, is that Christians do not invoke the name of God at slaughter. This issue has to be discussed in the light of the following verses:

"*He (Allah) has forbidden you ... the flesh of that animal over which any name other than that of Allah has been invoked...*" (Qur'ān 2:173).

This verse was repeated in 16:115, while verse 5:4 contains the additional prohibition of flesh of that

"*which has been slaughtered on the idolatrous altars.*"

These prohibitions do not apply to Christians, as they do not invoke the name of any deity when they slaughter their food animals, neither do they make any idolatrous offerings. The moot point of this issue revolves round the following verses of the Qur'ān:

"*So, eat of meats on which Allah's name has been pronounced, if you have faith in His revelations. And what reason have you that you should not eat of that on which Allah's name has been pronounced – when He has already distinguished for you the things which are forbidden ...*" (Qur'ān 6:118, 119)[26]

"*Hence eat not of that on which Allah's name has not been pronounced, for this would be an infraction* [Fisq] ..." (Qur'ān 6:121).

Verses 118 and 119 give Muslims permission to eat meat of those animals on which Allah's name *has been* pronounced; and verse 121 categorically forbids the eating of that on which it *has not been* pronounced. We know that Christians generally do not invoke God's or anyone else's name at the time of slaughter. Hence, according to the above verses, meat slaughtered by them must be unlawful for Muslims. However, verse 5:5, quoted earlier in this chapter, declares their meat as lawful, and this has been posing a serious theological problem for Muslims. It is inconceivable for Muslims even to think of any contradiction in the revealed word of God or to acquiesce to any suggestion that any passage of the Qur'ān abrogates another. Even the explanation that the meat slaughtered by Christians was made lawful in verse 5:5 because they used to invoke the name of God during the early days of Christianity and that it was only later that they stopped doing so, does not hold good. Firstly, there is no conclusive evidence that they used to invoke the name of God in those days. Secondly, as stated earlier in connection with pork, God's comprehension of the future is for perpetuity. This obviously, is a serious theological subject of inquiry for those millions of Muslims who wish to discipline their lives according to the tenets of Islam.

The question of whether the meat of an animal slaughtered without pronouncing the name of God is lawful or not has been under discussion since the early days of Islam. Erudites such as 'Aṭā' ibn Yasār, al-Qāsim ibn Mukhaymarah, al-Sha'bī, al-Zuhrī, Makḥūl and Rabī'ah opine that it is lawful. Opposed to that is the opinion of savants such as the Imām 'Alī, 'Ā'ishah, 'Ubādah ibn al-Ṣāmit and Abū al-Dardā'. However, the majority of classical doctors of law (*Fuqahā'*) believe that such meat becomes lawful by pronouncing the name of God before eating. Until recently the problem used to be, more or less, of theoretical concern but, with the current migration of millions of Muslims to Christian-dominated countries, it has become a quandary of practical implications which cannot be solved by popular sentiment. Perhaps a discussion, in the light of the following Qur'ānic commentaries and *Aḥādīth*, would help readers in finding their own answers:

Imām 'Alī ibn Abī Ṭālib[27] said, on the authority of the Holy Prophet[(s)]:

> "May God curse those who slay without repeating the name of God, in the same manner as the polytheists did in the name of their idols."[28]

Imām Mālik holds that the invocation of God's name is obligatory for Muslims only. If a Christian or Jew does not invoke the name, the meat is still lawful for a Muslim. Ibn 'Abbās also believes that the law to invoke God's name is not obligatory for Christians and Jews.

ʿAṭāʾ, al-Awzāʿī, Makḥūl and al-Layth ibn Saʿd hold that the verse 'the food of those who have received the Scripture is lawful for you' has rendered lawful 'that which has been immolated to other than Allah'. Al-Awzāʿī says that one may eat of the game hunted by a Christian even if one hears the Christian taking the name of Christ over his dog as he sets it off. Makḥūl says that there is no harm in eating of the animals which the People of the Book slaughter for their churches and synagogues and religious ceremonies.[29]

"...the reciting of *Tasmiyah* at the time of slaughtering of the animal [for reasons other than food] is not a necessary concomitant, although a desirable one. The reciting of the *Tasmiyah* described in the above-mentioned verses refers only to the slaughtering of animals for the sake of food... ."

"It should be observed that if someone has eaten the meat of an animal slaughtered for food without reciting the name of God on it, no learned doctor of religion has ever considered this a transgression or sin (*Fisq*)."

"It is related from the Imāms Shāfiʿī, Ibn Ḥanbal and Mālik that the *Tasmiyah* is not necessary [for non-Muslims]. Imām Abū Ḥanīfah held that it was essential. Nevertheless, he also says that, if the slaughterer forgot the *Tasmiyah* then the meat was quite all right and permissible to eat."[30]

Meat slaughtered by the People of the Book without reciting the name of God is, according to Imām Abū Ḥanīfah, undesirable or hateful to eat. This view is supported by various Imāms, such as Nawawī, Abū Yūsuf, Zufar, Muḥammad and Nakhʿī.[31]

Imām Shafiʿī opines that the food of the People of the Book is lawful for Muslims whether they have invoked the name of God or not. However he believes that, if it were known that the slaughterer has invoked the name of someone other than God, the food becomes unlawful for Muslims.

Al-Zuhrī (a Companion of the Holy Prophet[(s)]) said: "There is no harm in [eating the meat of] an animal slaughtered by a Christian. If you hear him [the slaughterer] invoking the name of someone other than Allah, do not eat it, but if you do not hear him, then Allah has made it lawful for you and He knew of their *Kufr*, i.e. Allah knew that they [the Christians] did not believe in Islam."

Ibn ʿAbbās, a prominent authority on Islam, while commenting on verse 5:6, confirms the above verdict and explains in clear words that this verse means that the animals slaughtered by the People of the Book are lawful for Muslims to eat provided the name of anyone other than that of Allah has not been invoked at the slaughter of the animal.[32]

According to Ibn Kathīr, the People of the Book also consider as unlawful the meat of an animal slaughtered in the name of idols or deities, even though their concept of God may be different in certain details from that of Muslims.[33]

According to the greatest authority of them all on *Ḥadīth*, Imām al-Bukhārī, the meat becomes unlawful only if the name of anyone other than that of God is invoked. However, he goes on to add that it becomes lawful if God's name (*Tasmiyah*) is pronounced afterwards, i.e. before eating.

> "If the slaughterer was heard invoking a name other than that of Allah, the meat was not to be eaten; but if it was not so heard, then it was lawful for Muslims to eat".[34]

Imām Fakhr al-Dīn Rāzī, commenting on verse 6:121 says:

> "That over which any name other than that of Allah has been invoked means the animals slaughtered by the worshippers of idols, which they used to slaughter as offerings to their idols."[35] Qāḍī al-Bayḍāwī agrees with this interpretation of this verse and says that it means "that meat over which the name of an idol has been invoked at the time of slaughter."[36]

It is obvious that, while some Imāms and doctors of law (*Fuqahāʾ*) differ with each other in matters of detail, they are agreed on the point that the meat of any animal on which the name of an idol or deity has been invoked is unlawful for Muslims.

There is another point of detail on which Muslim authorities are not unanimous. What is the position if a Muslim slaughterer omits to pronounce *Takbīr*? The majority of jurists (*Fuqahā'*) agree that the meat is lawful if the omission is unintentional. Imām Shāfi'ī is of the opinion that, although it is not lawful to omit the *Takbīr* intentionally and that the eating of such a meat is reprehensible (*Makrūh*), yet it cannot be declared as unlawful (*Ḥarām*), provided that the other conditions of slaughter have been carried out rightly. Imām Mālik believes that the meat of such an animal is unlawful even if the omission of *takbīr* is unintentional. Imām Abū Ḥanīfah takes the mid-course that such meat is lawful, if the omission is unintentional; and unlawful, if it is intentional.

According to the following *Ḥadīth*, the meat of an animal which has been slaughtered without invoking God's name becomes lawful for Muslims if the consumer pronounces the name of God before eating – whatever the circumstances and reasons for the omission may be:

> "A group of people said to the Prophet: 'some people bring the meat and we do not know whether they have mentioned Allah's name or not while slaughtering the animal'. The Prophet said, 'mention Allah's name on the meat and eat it'."[37]

It is argued by some that the people who are mentioned in this *Ḥadīth* as selling meat to Muslims were recent converts to Islam and, although Muslims, were of doubtful faith. If this kind of principle were to be accepted, then one should scrutinise and ascertain the probity, the faith (*Īmān*), and proficiency in the Islamic Law of every Muslim butcher and slaughterman before eating the meat of an animal slaughtered by him. It is not easy to imagine what kind of world it would become if religious discipline were to be imposed in that spirit. There is a precept in Islam that, in case of unintentional omission of God's name before any act, one should mention it whenever one is reminded of it after the event in these words: "In the name of God – both for the antecedence and the subsequence" (*Bismillāh Awwaluh wa Ākhiruh*). However, these days it is a practice more honoured in the breach than the observance.

Muslims are supposed to invoke Allah's name before eating, drinking or doing anything. It is what they call in English "saying grace" in these words: "In the name of Allah Who is Beneficent and Merciful" (*Bismillāhi-r-Raḥmāni-r-Raḥīm*). Some people have misunderstood the significance of the above *Ḥadīth* by equating the normal grace with the invocation of God's name before slaughter which comprises two phrases. One is the invocation of Allah's name (*Bismillāh*), i.e. "in the name of Allah" and the second is the glorification of Allah (*Allāhu Akbar*), meaning "God is the Greatest". When the Holy Prophet[s] was asked by his Companions in the above *Ḥadīth* about the meat slaughtered by people who might not have carried out the act of slaughter (*Tadhkiyah*) and the recitation of God's name (*Tasmiyah* and *Takbīr*) according to the Islamic prescript, his advice was not to discard the meat because of that reason but to eat the meat after invoking God's name in the same phraseology which is used at the time of slaughter. This *Ḥadīth* implies that: when a Muslim is in doubt whether the animal was slaughtered according to the *Sharī'ah* law or not, he should make it lawful by pronouncing God's name (*Tasmiyah*) before eating it.*

THE RELATIVE SIGNIFICANCE OF BLEEDING AND THE INVOCATION OF GOD'S NAME

It was mentioned earlier that the invocation of God's name (*Takbīr*) is considered more important than the act or method of slaughter. There is no disputing the fact that, according to the dietetic laws of *Sharī'ah*, the flesh of game hunted for food is lawful (*Ḥalāl*) if the *Takbīr* has been pronounced before shooting or setting the dogs and birds of prey after it – even though the

* However, many Muslims would not eat the meat of an animal on which the name of God has not been pronounced at the time of the slaughter. To invoke the name of God (*Tasmiyah*) at the time of eating, according to them, does not make it lawful for consumption – Ed.

animal dies before the hunter has had a chance to slaughter it. Islam has laid great emphasis on bleeding the animal to render the meat hygienically pure as food. In the Islamic terminology, the very act of slaughter (*Dhabḥ*) is called 'the process of purification and cleansing' (*Tadhkiyah*). In spite of all this emphasis on bleeding, the law of slaughter is mollified in the case of hunting, while the hunter still remains bound by the covenant of *Takbīr*. It is very important for Muslims to appreciate the reason underlying this relaxation of the law. In the case of animals slain by hunting, Islam is more concerned with the fundamental requirement that no life should be allowed to go to waste, rather than with the formalistic enactment of decrees.

There are a large number of Muslims living in the tropical and subtropical savannahs where their main source of meat is hunting. Many a time such people do not get a chance to bleed the animal and carry out the normal *Tadhkiyah* before it is dead. Unlike the Mosaic law,[38] Islam allows Muslims to procure their food by hunting. It cannot, therefore, be said that the relaxation of the law of normal slaughter is by way of an exception – it is a regular feature of the law as the following Qur'ānic passages show:

> "*They ask you [O Muḥammad!] what is lawful to them as food. Tell them: 'Lawful unto you are [all] things good and pure; and what your trained animals and birds of prey catch in the manner directed to you by Allah. So eat of that which they catch for you and pronounce the name of Allah over it – Allah is Swift in reckoning.*" (Qur'ān 5:4)

> "*And you are allowed to hunt the aquatic game; its use as food is a provision both for those of you who are at home and those who are on a journey ... .*" (Qur'ān 5:96)

There is a consensus among Muslim theologians that hunting is allowed in Islam only for the basic necessities of life and that it may be done with animals or birds of prey, with bows and arrows, or with other weapons including firearms.

"Abū Tha'labah, a Companion of the Holy Prophet(s), narrates that the Prophet(s) said, in reply to some questions, that you can eat an animal which you have hunted with your bow or with your dog, whom you have trained as a hunting dog, provided you have mentioned the name of Allah on it and provided it has no stench."[39]

> "'Adiyy ibn Ḥātim narrated that Allah's Messenger said to him: 'When you set off your dog, mention Allah's name, and if it catches anything and you come up to it while it is still alive, cut its throat; if you come up to it when the dog has killed it but not eaten any of it, eat it' … ." For further clarification, 'Adiyy ibn Ḥātim told Allah's Messenger that he set off trained dogs, and the Prophet replied, 'Eat what they catch for you.' 'Adiyy asked if that applied even if the dogs had killed the game. The Prophet replied that it did."[40]

Many other such *Aḥādīth* leave no doubt that a hunted animal is lawful to eat, even if it dies unslaughtered and that it makes no difference how long it has been dead – as long as its flesh has not putrefied and is hygienically edible. For example:

> "'Adiyy ibn Ḥātim narrates that he said to the Messenger of God(s): 'I shoot at game and find it dead the next day with my arrow in it.' The Messenger of God(s) replied: 'When you know that your arrow killed it and you see no mark of a beast of prey on the animal, you may eat it.'"[41]

It has never been the purport of Islamic laws to be observed as ceremonial rites. Great care has been taken to keep them within the bounds of practicability – to make them congruous with all situations and circumstances of human needs. Muhammad Asad, the learned translator of the Qur'ān of the 20th century, while commenting on verse 6:119 which allows the eating of any lawful meat on which God's name has been pronounced, says: "The purpose of this and the following verse is .... a reminder that the observance of such laws should not be made an end in itself and an object of ritual: and this is the reason why these two verses have been placed in the midst of a discourse on God's transcendental unity and the way of man's faith. The 'errant views' [fancies = *Ahwā'ahum*] spoken of in 119 are such as lay stress on artificial rituals and taboos rather than on spiritual values."[42]

REFERENCES AND NOTES

1. For details cf. *al-Ḥalāl wa'l-Ḥarām fi'l-Islām* (in Arabic); Yūsuf al-Qaraḍāwī; Maktabat Wahbah, Cairo; 1977. English translation: *The Lawful and the Prohibited in Islam*; Kamal El-Helbawy and others; American Trust Publications, 10900 W. Washington Street, Indianapolis, IN 46231, USA. Also *al-Fiqh* (In Arabic) (The Islamic Jurisprudence); 'Abd al-Raḥmān Khallāf; Maktabat al-Sha'b, Cairo.
2. The four Schools of Thought were established by the following Imāms within the first about one and a half centuries of the Islamic era. The only purpose of these Schools was the codification of the Islamic jurisprudence (*Fiqh*):

    1. Imām Abū Ḥanīfah al-Nu'mān ibn Thābit. Born at Baṣrah, (699-767 A.C.).
    2. Imām Mālik ibn Anas. Born at Madina (713-795 A.C.).
    3. Imām Abū 'Abdullāh Muḥammad ibn Idrīs al-Shāfi'ī. Born in Palestine (767-821 A.C.)
    4. Imām Aḥmad ibn Ḥanbal. Born in Baghdād (781-858 A.C.).

3. cf. *Commentary of the Qur'ān* by Ibn Jurayj. Also cf. *al-Tafsīr al-Kabīr* by Imām Fakhr al-Dīn al-Rāzī, (hereafter referred to as Rāzī).
4. For the literal meaning of *Istaqsimū* and *Azlām*, cf: Shaykh Abū'l-Qāsim al-Ḥusayn al-Rāghib in *al-Mufradāt fī Gharīb al-Qur'ān* (hereafter referred to as Rāghib); A dictionary of the Qur'ān entitled: *Arabic-English Lexicon* by Edward William Lane.
5. cf. Rāzī. (See Ref. No. 3).
6. cf. Rāghib (See Ref. 4).
7. Bukhārī, 72:22.
8. The Sabians mentioned in the Qur'ān as *Ṣābi'īn* in three places (2:62; 5:72; 22:17) are different people from the Biblical Sabians, perhaps deriving their name from *Sheba.* The Qur'ānic Ṣābi'īn were an offshoot of Christianity. *Encyclopaedia Britannica*

describes them as "Christians of St. John the Baptist". In the early Arab literature they have also been called 'those who wash themselves' (*al-Mughtasilah*). The Biblical Sabians seem to be a people of Southern Arabia whose kingdom was at its height in the 5th century B.C. They were prosperous businessmen, very rich and worshipped heavenly bodies. As polytheists, they could not have been called by the Qur'ān as the possessors of Scripture or the People of the Book *(Ahl al-Kitāb)*.

9. See Ref. No. 2.
10. Sayyid Sabiq; *Fiqh al-Sunnah* (Islamic Jurisprudence based on the practice of the Holy Prophet[s]). Vol.3, p.264 (hereafter referred to as "Sābiq"), Dār al-Kitāb al-'Arabī, Beirut 1971.
11. See "Sābiq", Ref. No. 12; p.298.
12. Sarakhsī has gone down in history with the title *Shams al-A'immah* (the sunshine of Muslim nations); *al-Mabsūṭ*. (The word 'ALWAYS' capitalised by the writer).
13. Abū Ḥayyān al-Gharnāṭī (the famous 14th century A.C. commentator of the Qur'ān; *al-Baḥr al-Muḥīṭ*, Vol. III, p.431.
14. The Muftī of Jordan as quoted by: *al-Muslimūn*; Geneva, June 1964, pp.108-111.
15. The Urdu Magazine *Burhān*; Pakistan, 1964.
16. Shaykh 'Abd al-Wahhāb Khallāf, as quoted in the Arabic Magazine: *Liwā' al-Islām*, Cairo, April-May, 1949.
17. Dr. 'Abdullāh al-'Abbādī; "*Qurbānīs in Islamic Law*" (in Arabic); pp.64-67.
18. Dr. 'Abd al-'Azīz al-Khayyāṭ, Dean of the Faculty of Islamic Law, University of Jordan; *Report on Food* and *Slaughtered Animals in Islam*; pp.35-44.
19. Sir Sayyid Aḥmad Khān; *Musāfirān-e-London*; Lahore, Pakistan; 1961; p.74.
20. *Al-Muslimūn*; Geneva; July 1964; p.53.
21. *The Times*, London. 29 July 1985.
22. Report on the Welfare of Livestock when Slaughtered by Religious Methods; Farm Animal Welfare Council, H.M. Stationery (London) Book Ref. 262, 1985, Para. 27, p.9 (hereafter referred to as "Report FAWC").
23. Report FAWC Book Ref. 262; (See Ref. No. 22) paras. 66-69, pp. 17, 18.
24. Report FAWC Book Ref 262; (See Ref. No. 22) para. 90, p.34.
25. *The Meaning of the Glorious Qur'ān;* Marmaduke Pickthall; 1957; footnote 2, Chapt 22, verse 34, p.341.
26. Verses 5:4, 5, preceding the verse 5:6, explain in some detail what is unlawful to eat and what is lawful (*Ṭayyibāt*).
27. Imām 'Alī was the son-in-law of the Holy Prophet[s] and the fourth Caliph of Islam (656-661 A.C.).

28. *Mishkāt al-Maṣābīḥ*, Book XVIII, Chapt. 1, as quoted in *The Dictionary of Islam* by Patrick Hughes, p.697.
29. As quoted by Abū A'lā Mawdūdī, *Tarjumān al-Qur'ān*, 1959.
30. *Al-Tāj fī Uṣūl al-Ḥadīth*, Cairo, Vol. III, p.110. (For details about the four Imāms, see Ref. No.2.)
31. cf. Abū Ḥayyān al-Andalusī; *al-Baḥr al-Muḥīṭ*; Vol. IV; p.131.
32. *Musnad* of Aḥmad; Vol. 1. p.302.
33. Ibn Kathīr, Vol. III, p.19.
34. Bukhārī, 72:20-22 Abū 'Abdullāh Muḥammad ibn Ismā'īl al-Bukhārī (774-836 A.C.) is the compiler of the most authentic book of *Ḥadīth* named after him as *Ṣaḥīḥ al-Bukhārī*.
35. cf. "Rāzī" (see Ref. No. 3.)
36. cf. *Anwār al-Tanzīl wa Asrār al-Ta'wīl* (Commentary of the Qur'ān) in Arabic; Qāḍī Abū Sa'īd 'Abdullāh ibn 'Umar al-Bayḍāwī.
37. Narrated by 'Ā'ishah, the wife of the Holy Prophet(s). Bukhārī, 72:22 English translation Vol. VII, p.302.
38. cf. *Landau*, 1770, p.104.
39. Bukhārī, 72:4. Also Muslim.
40. a) Bukhārī 7:2 and 7:7, Muslim and Abū Dāwūd, Also: James Robson's English translation of *Mishkāt al Maṣābīḥ;* Sh. Muhammad Ashraf, Lahore, Pakistan; 1963; Vol. 3, p. 873. (hereafter referred to as "Robson") Also: *Kitāb al-Ṣayd wa'l Dhabā'iḥ wa mā Yu'kalu min al-Ḥayawān*; English translation: *Book of Game and the Animals Which May be Slaughtered And the Animals that May be Eaten;* Chapt. DCCCX on "*Hunting with the Help of Dogs*"; Ḥadīth No. 4732.

    b) For details about the training of hunting dogs etc. see: *Hidāyah*; 'Abdullāh ibn 'Umar; Vol. IV, p.86.
41. Abū Dāwūd, as quoted in *Mishkāt al-Maṣābīḥ*; "Robson", p.873 (See Ref. No. 37).
42. *The Message of the Qur'ān*; Muhammad Asad; Dar al-Andalus, Gibraltar, 1980; Footnote No. 104, p.190.

INDEX